DBT Therapy Workbook for Teens

A Friendly Skills Guide to Manage Anxiety, Stress, Depression, and BPD. Regulate and Understand your Emotions Through Practical Exercises

By

Kardas Publishing

The trademarks that are used are without any consent, and the publication of the trademark is without permission or backing by the trademark owner. All trademarks and brands within this book are for clarifying purposes only and are the owned by the owners themselves, not affiliated with this document.

Contents

Don't Worry!

You are not alone...

Introduction

Why are so many of us turning to self-destructive and self-harming habits?

You may already be aware that many people purposefully self-harm and suffer physical hurt, so no, you are not insane or strange. There are several reasonable explanations for why people harm themselves in multiple ways. However, it can help if you recognize that this behavior is not good or beneficial in the long run.

So, first and foremost, congratulations on realizing that self-destructive behavior are not something you would like to keep in your daily existence.

If you have picked up this book, you have probably been through one or more horrible events that have had a lasting influence on your life. You are probably looking for relief from pain and symptoms that interfere with your capacity to regulate emotions, develop relationships, and fully engage in life. Experiencing a terrible incident may be emotionally draining, isolating, and terrifying. You could be doing considerable efforts to avoid feeling worried and restricting your capacity to live a healthy and productive life.

There is still a lot to understand about our minds, and there is still a lot of work that needs to be done when it relates to emotions. Dialectical Behavior Therapy (DBT) is an evidence-based treatment that teaches people how to learn and apply new skills and methods to live the lives they enjoy. DBT was created keeping Borderline Personality Disorder in mind. However, it can help persons with Post-Traumatic Stress Disorder (PTSD), suicidality, self-harm, drug abuse, anxiety, and eating disorders, among other mental health conditions.

A one-year commitment is required for a basic DBT treatment. Shorter programs, often known as "DBT-informed programs," utilize elements of DBT's techniques and can be quite beneficial for some people. In this workbook, I have added practical activities that contribute to the understanding of emotions, the acceptance of tough feelings, the acquisition of skills to handle them, the ability to make changes for the betterment of one's life, and a rise in motivation. These exercises and activities will teach you coping strategies in your emotional time.

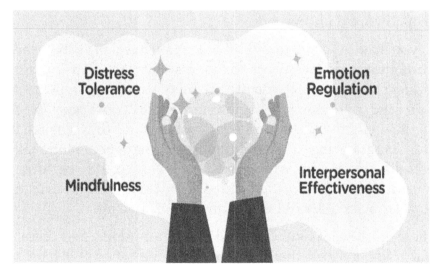

In DBT, we feel that persons who engage in mental and behavioral problems do so for the two reasons given below.

Do you tend to feel things more frequently and intensely than others? Do others tell you that you tend to overreact to situations? That you are a crybaby? If this describes you, feel confident that you have played no part in the situation. So, the first reason is that you are the person who lives with greater sensitivity than the others. This increased sensitivity might be due to genes passed down from your parents, a mental health issue you were born with, or troubles your mother experienced while she was expecting.

However, this is only one aspect of why people self-harm and do self-destructive actions. The setting in which you grow up is very important. Our environment has a significant part in our development. For persons who are being mistreated or neglected while growing up is the second reason. However, you do not have to be abused to engage in harmful activities. One of the most prevalent environmental variables that correlate to persons' leaning to self-harm and self-destructive behaviors is growing up in a rejecting environment. They are told that their inner experiences are incorrect, such as their feelings and thoughts.

The conclusion here is that you are not to blame for developing the issues that have led to self-harming and self-destructive behaviors. It is a mix of your vulnerability and the environment you grew up in, which has not provided you with the emotional support you require. So, no, it is not your fault, and yes, it is up to you to strive to improve your situation. You are not the only one in this situation. It is critical to recognize that life-threatening and traumatic experiences are unfortunately prevalent but survival and thriving are achievable. The first step in recovering from trauma is to figure out how to deal with your symptoms. If you suffer from addictive behaviors, this workbook is for you.

This book is intended to assist you on your path of discovery and healing. Whether you are new to recovery or have been in recovery for a long time, it will assist you in improving your social and emotional development and preventing relapse. The purpose of this workbook is to help you:

- Reduce or eliminate the behaviors to which you are addicted and provide you with healthy coping techniques.

- Talk about what's causing your addictions and how you can get help where it is needed the most.

- To enhance your relationships and ensure long-term emotional development, teach good interpersonal, self-awareness, and leadership abilities.

- Give you hands-on, simple workouts and activities to help you achieve the life you want.

This book's material breaks down important skills and lessons into pleasant and manageable chunks that you may go through with your family or therapist. Professionals understand that learning by practicing produces the most solid and long-lasting results. The book's framework includes the opportunity to practice these abilities in several ways. It covers all important areas of DBT skills training, including improving self-awareness and awareness of your surroundings. Life is difficult; it is something you already know. However, you are not powerless or locked in your emotional battle. You may anticipate your reactions to feelings to change if you put in the effort to practice the strategies in this workbook. That is because the essential skills you will learn here may affect the result of any disagreement and can change the trajectory of your relationships, irrespective of heredity or childhood suffering. Remember that the work you put into this healing process determines the results you will get.

It is entirely up to you how much effort you put in and how much benefit you derive from this approach. There is a reason to be hopeful; all you have to do now is continue reading. You are embarking on a journey of healing that will take you away from addiction and toward harmony.

Let's relax our muscles before we get started with our journey. Here I have a relaxing exercise for you.

You will obtain a powerful sense of relaxation by stretching and releasing the muscles across your body. Muscular relaxation will allow you to detect feelings of muscle tension, which will assist you in noticing worry.

Relax and take a seat or lie down in a comfortable posture. You will stretch your muscles firmly, but not to the level of strain, in each of the bodily areas indicated below. Tension should be held for ten seconds, and you should pay special attention to how it works. Then, when you let go of the tension, note how the sensation of relaxation varies from that of tension.

Shoulders

Squeeze and lift your shoulders towards your head, then let them fall.

Arms

Raise hands and press them toward your head, then release them.

Thighs

Pull your legs tightly together, then release them.

Face

Pull your facial structure together in the middle of your face, then release.

Torso

Pull in your abdomen, then let go of the tension and allow it to relax.

Back

Squeeze your shoulders back together, and then let go.

Feet

Curl your toes into the feet firmly, then relax them.

Calves

Stretch or extend your feet, then relax them.

Hands

Curl your fingertips into your palm, form a fist, and then loosen your fingers.

Full Body

Squeeze all of your muscles tightly, then release the strain.

Now you are relaxed. Let's get started with the treatment.

Chapter 1: Introduction to DBT

Dialectical Behavior Therapy (DBT) is a modified form of cognitive-behavioral therapy. Its primary objectives are to assist young individuals in enjoying the present time, building healthy stress coping strategies, managing their mental illness, and enhancing their social interaction. DBT was created to treat Borderline Personality Disorder (BPD), but it is now being used to treat various other mental illnesses. It can assist persons who have trouble regulating their emotions or engage in self-destructive behavior. Post-traumatic stress disorder (PTSD) is sometimes treated with this form of therapy. Dr. Marsha Linehan and colleagues created DBT in the late 1980s after discovering that cognitive-behavioral therapy (CBT) alone did not function as effectively as predicted in individuals with BPD. Dr. Linehan and her colleagues modified approaches and created a treatment to match the people's specific requirements. DBT was created keeping BPD in mind, although it might also be beneficial for:

- Suicidal behavior
- Substance use disorder
- Post-traumatic stress disorder (PTSD)
- Attention-deficit/hyperactivity disorder (ADHD)
- Obsessive-compulsive disorder (OCD)
- Bipolar disorder
- Non-suicidal self-injury
- Major depressive disorder
- Borderline personality disorder (BPD)
- Generalized anxiety disorder (GAD)
- Eating disorders

1.1 Basic Understanding of DBT

The term "dialectical" refers to the concept of combining two opposites in treatment that are; acceptance and transformation. Both produce greater outcomes than either of them working alone. DBT's goal is to help you:

- Accept and understand your challenging feelings while teaching you how to handle them.
- Become capable of making great life changes
- Trying to comprehend how two seemingly opposing things may both be true

Accepting yourself and altering your behavior may appear to be mutually opposed. However, DBT emphasizes that you can attain both of these objectives simultaneously. The four sections of a basic DBT are as follows:

1. Individual counseling
2. Group skill development
3. Coaching over the phone
4. Group of consultation

Patients commit to practicing new abilities by doing homework. This includes keeping track of over 40 emotions, impulses, actions, and abilities, such as lying, personality, and consciousness, using daily "personal journal cards." DBT is a multistage, sensible approach:

Stage 1: Addresses the most self-destructive behaviors, such as attempted suicide and self-injury.

Stage 2: Emotional control, stress management, and effective communication are among the abilities addressed in this stage.

Stage 3: Improved interactions and self-esteem are the main goals of this stage.

Stage 4: Encourages more pleasure and closeness in relationships.

1.2 How Does DBT Work?

DBT works by focusing on four different strategies to improve life skills:

1. **Mindfulness:** The process of discovering your inner focus to become more aware of oneself and others, as well as paying attention to the current moment.

2. **Emotion Regulation** is recognizing, classifying, and regulating emotions.

3. **Tolerance** for extreme emotions such as anger without reacting impulsively or relieving discomfort through self-injury or drug dependence.

4. **Interpersonal Effectiveness**: Navigating conflicts and behaving assertively.

Each of the strategies mentioned above has been discussed in the following chapters, and several exercises have also been given to assist DBT.

DBT's ultimate purpose is to assist you in living a life that you cherish. Each person's definition of a meaningful and fulfilling life is different. This is why therapists assist people in focusing on what matters to them. Thus, the correct strategy to determine if DBT is appropriate for you is to speak with a DBT-trained therapist. To assess if DBT is a suitable fit for you, they'll look at your symptoms, clinical history, and therapeutic expectations.

1.3 Difference Between DBT and CBT

Considering their identical titles, is there a difference between CBT and DBT, and can one be more effective than the other?

Continue reading to discover the distinctions between CBT and DBT, as well as how to choose which will be most beneficial to you.

Psychotherapy is one of the most effective treatments for various mental disorders. Cognitive Behavioral Therapy is among the most frequent therapy methods. CBT, often known as talk therapy, concentrates on talking about your difficulties to help you reframe your thinking. Suppose you feel that negative thinking is constantly controlling you. In that case, you could imagine like, "I am a loser," "I'm incapable of doing anything correctly," "If people realize who they truly are, no one will like them." Cognitive Behavioral Therapy (CBT) can teach you how to use logic and reason to take control of your ideas rather than allowing them to dominate you. Cognitive-behavioral therapy identifies and changes harmful thought patterns and encourages good behavioral changes. CBT is founded on the premise that our ideas and behaviors impact our moods; therefore, changing how we think about and react to circumstances can help us feel better. CBT is an umbrella term for a variety of treatments with similar qualities. CBT therapists often use a talk therapy approach that includes key guiding elements.

On the other hand, Standard CBT does not help treat all mental diseases. CBT focuses on assisting you in changing problematic thought and behavior patterns. Dialectical Behavior Treatment is another prevalent kind of therapy. DBT is a more particular type of CBT that emphasizes assisting people who have intense emotional reactions to engage with their surroundings in a less stressful, healthier manner.

DBT varies from CBT in the sense that it also emphasizes accepting yourself as you are. Suicidal and other self-destructive behaviors may be treated with DBT. It teaches patients how to cope with bad behaviors and modify them. DBT is also more likely to incorporate group work than CBT. A DBT therapist will want you to fight hard to create good chances and support yourself. While DBT is designed to help individuals realize the discomfort and pain they are experiencing while feeling secure and "fine" and encouraged to select healthy behaviors over impulsive or dangerous ones. Clients are taught to recognize triggers outside of themselves and link them with a positive coping strategy or reaction, while some focus is on dealing with emotions.

DBT has been developed to assist people who have been diagnosed with borderline personality disorder. Rather than attempting to reason or speak through the challenges that people are having, DBT focuses on helping them modify their behavior patterns. This aids people who have acquired habits of high emotional reactions and impulsive behaviors in reaction to overwhelming emotions of anguish and humiliation - the sensation of walking through a world full of blades, as described by patients. For people who deal with self-harming habits like cutting and prolonged suicidal thoughts, DBT is typically the most successful therapy. DBT approaches work effectively for sexual trauma sufferers as well.

With so many treatment choices available, it can be difficult to determine which treatments will be most beneficial to you. CBT and DBT are two of the most prominent therapeutic techniques that have been demonstrated to benefit people with a variety of mental diseases.

Benefits of Dialectical Behavioral Therapy

In DBT, the client and therapist work together to reconcile the seeming conflict between self-acceptance and transformation to help the therapist make good changes. Offering reinforcement is a part of this journey, making individuals more prepared to collaborate and less likely to be distressed by the prospect of change. In practice, the therapist confirms that a person's behaviors "make logical sense" in the framework of their circumstances without actually agreeing that they are the best way to solve an issue.

- Change and acknowledgment: You will discover techniques for accepting and tolerating your life circumstances, feelings, and yourself. You will also gain skills that will assist you in making good adjustments in your conduct and interactions with others.

- **Behavioral:** You will learn to identify issues and detrimental behavior patterns, then substitute them with healthier and more productive ones.

- **Cognitive:** You will concentrate on modifying ineffective or harmful attitudes and beliefs.

- **Collaboration:** You will learn how to successfully communicate and collaborate as a group.

- **Skill sets:** You will get new talents by learning new skills.

- **Support:** You will be taught to discover and enhance your positive skills and traits.

Effectiveness of Dialectical Behavior Therapy

People can discover efficient strategies to control and express powerful emotions with this approach to treatment since it can help them improve their coping abilities. DBT is also beneficial regardless of age, gender, gender identification, sexual preference, or race/ethnicity.

DBT is beneficial in treating borderline personality disorder (BPD) and lowering the risk of suicides in people with BPD. According to one research, more than 75% of persons with BPD no longer fit the clinical criteria for the disorder after a year of therapy.

For suicidal behavior, another research revealed that therapies that included skills training as a therapeutic component were more successful in decreasing suicidality.

For other mental illnesses: While most DBT work has concentrated on its usefulness for persons with borderline personality disorder who have suicidal and self-harming thoughts, the therapy may also benefit those with other mental health issues. According to a study, this sort of therapy seems to be useful in treating PTSD, anxiety, and nervousness.

1.4 True Stories of Teenagers

To satisfy your concerns about DBT's effectiveness, I am writing success stories from some of my clients who recovered from mental illnesses using DBT.

Anonymous Patient

The patient had been receiving mental health treatments in some form or another since she was approximately 14 years old, with varying levels of success. There were many amazing highs and many startling lows in her life. She felt something was not right with how she dealt with her problems, but she did not know what it was or how to fix it. She was reviewed and identified with Borderline Personality Disorder (BPD) and Post Traumatic Stress Disorder after several months with a diagnosis of major depression. The diagnosis of BPD was upsetting to her. Despite the phrase and accompanying stigma, it was a relief to the family that there was therapy present in the form of Dialectical Behavior Therapy (DBT).

Two therapists examined her for the DBT treatment. She had to be honest and open about her thoughts and actions. It was a difficult and unpleasant situation for her. She attended two-hour weekly training groups and fortnightly one-on-one sessions.

She was hesitant to visit the skills lessons because she used to find any type of therapy unpleasant. Still, after some time, she decided to treat the activities group more like a college course, which helped her focus and absorb more information from the meetings. The skills group frequently triggered her, and she was unable to participate or had to leave early in several situations, but the therapists were supportive and pushed her to stay, which she did for 40 weeks.

She enjoyed the skills group because it focused on developing new abilities to cope with emergencies and better methods to analyze her emotions and actions rather than the traumas she experienced. She learned things that she wished she had known as a youngster, such as affirming herself in particular situations and expressing herself in more constructive ways. She also learned to employ mindfulness to manage her emotions and practice tolerance over time.

The one-on-one sessions she had were quite beneficial. Her therapist was able to assist her in comprehending and using the DBT techniques she was acquiring. Her most important lesson was recognizing that she could also fail and this recognition along with continual practice, was the key to adopting DBT. The consistency of the therapy was crucial in managing some of her most severe BPD symptoms, as she had described.

Then she felt like she had a better grasp of her life's events. When things got difficult or her mood got out of hand, she had a toolkit of options to consider before reverting to previous, destructive behaviors.

She had better understood her diagnoses and habits, attempting to see things from a new perspective. She said she would not call herself "better," but she would describe herself as "doing better." Her friends and family observed a favorable difference in her attitude and conduct, and she felt more capable of communicating with the people in her life. She pictured herself in the future the way she had never imagined before the treatment.

Annie, Age 20

As she was transferred from one specialist to the next, Annie characterized her life as a "living nightmare." She was offered several psychoactive drugs. Her pills had horrible adverse effects that only made her depression worse. Annie discovered a technique to self-medicate by using her mother's pain killers, and she developed an addiction to drugs over time.

Annie was a clinically complicated client who was twenty (20) years old, unmarried, and Caucasian. Severe Depression and Substance Abuse Disorder were her diagnoses.

Annie received mental health therapy in outpatient and intensive outpatient programs for three years. Annie's family had been helpful during this period, but they were powerless to help her because she struggled with her pain killers' addiction. Her severe sadness caused her to close down and isolate herself from her relatives.

Annie had gotten to the point where she couldn't get out of bed and was continuously shouting at her parents due to her depression. Annie's parents continued to look into inpatient facilities that worked with multiple diagnoses and provided evidence-based therapy.

While waiting for admittance approval to an inpatient institution, Annie's parents prepared her for a full psychiatric assessment. Annie was accepted into an inpatient program for young ladies between 18 and 28.

Dialectical Behavior Therapy was used in the therapy procedure. The first step in using DBT was identifying the problematic behavioral patterns at the root of Annie's problems, hindering her from succeeding in all areas of her life.

Annie's therapist worked with her to restructure her self-perception and how she perceived herself in connections with others, particularly her close family, and improved her interpersonal and self-management abilities. Overall, Annie's therapy was customized, with particular cognitive, behavioral, and systemic interventions to address her dysfunctional elements.

Annie struggled at first due to her sadness and inability to familiarize herself with the scheduled days in the milieu. She spent more time with her therapist to reconnect to DBT therapy and the objectives they agreed to achieve from the start.

Annie finished the inpatient program and kept meeting with an outpatient therapist once a week. As she was back at home, she continued to have monthly family meetings. She had stopped using pain medicine and returned to school. She chose to pursue a degree in English literature as she was interested in composing poetry.

Rachel, Age 33

Rachel used to self-harm regularly, but she had not done so in nearly six years (since right after she began DBT). she used to battle suicidal ideas and attempts, but it had been approximately three years since Rachel was hospitalized.

She could never stay at work because she used to have anxiety attacks, leave suddenly, or call off due to being hospitalized. Before DBT, Rachel could not have solid relationships, but she was in a happy, stable relationship after the therapy and preparing for her wedding. Rachel said, "I'm not ideal, and I've realized that I don't have to be a good, successful, and important person."

Rachel put forward a lot of effort to make her life worthwhile. She got the work that she enjoyed, where she could put her music degree to good use and gain expertise and confidence. She put a lot of effort into her friendships, family, and romantic relationships to maintain them healthy, secure, and mutually advantageous. DBT taught her how to shape her life into what she wanted it to be, rather than merely reacting to what happened around her. Rachel had complete control over her reactions, which was important to her. She continued to learn how to affirm herself and let go of things that were not good for her. She said, "I must say, this is the happiest and most peaceful I've ever been, and it's all thanks to the tools I learned in DBT!"

Chapter 2: Discovering the Inner Focus

Dialectic Behavior Therapy is a psychotherapy technique that focuses on habits that are frequently disadvantageous and are not useful in meeting one's needs in interactions and in general. My opinion is that the priority in this sort of treatment is on the behaviors that negatively influence an individual's life rather than the mental process, or underlying beliefs, that drive these actions. As a psychotherapist, my goal and ambition, is to draw attention to these fundamental basic beliefs that unknowingly drive our conditioned responses to ourselves as "the internal voice" and our loved ones in relationships. In my opinion and experience, identifying and seeing through these ideas gradually functions as a vital foundation toward releasing our inner negative thoughts and becoming least governed by these beliefs. This chapter will help you discover your inner focus with simple and easy-to-follow exercises and worksheets.

2.1 Role of Inner Focus

Validation, or acknowledging unpleasant emotions and events before attempting to alter them, is a core component of DBT. The change appears achievable when patients encounter negative ideas and feelings. Individuals can engage with their therapists to develop a rehabilitation plan by concentrating on their inner thoughts. As, one of my clients couldn't concentrate on her studies. We discussed her thinking flexibility and made some modifications to her study schedule. She worked for half an hour, then took a 10-minute break before returning to study for another half an hour. She discovered that she could achieve a lot more in two shorter periods.

Maybe you are puzzled why identifying inner focus is so critical. However, as American psychiatrist Dan Siegel puts it, if you cannot identify it, you will not be able to control it. Once you have identified it, you will be better equipped to determine what to do about your focus. Starting with verifying the emotion you are having, which is the next ability we will look at here. Let's look at an example to see why inner focus is significant.

After your workday is done, your supervisor insists that you continue on a project. You find yourself screaming or fighting to catch your breath all of a sudden. Alternatively, the kids are arguing, and you lose your patience, shouting at them to stop, and then you beat yourself up for losing your composure. You hide your emotions with your harmful distraction of preference because you do not know what to do with them.

Do not stress if this sounds similar; you are not the only one. We all deal with powerful emotional responses at times — it is simply a part of being human. However, the failure to control emotions in a healthy, efficient manner can be a chronic issue with several harmful consequences for other people. It is difficult to think about what you can do to assist yourself while your emotions are already high, so the first thing you should focus on is finding your concentration as soon as possible. Here are several quick-acting abilities that change your brain's chemistry. It is best to test them out before you are in an emotional scenario so you know how to utilize your attention to deal with it.

2.2 Exercises and Activities for Discovering Inner Focus

How many times have you hurried out the door and plan your day without giving it a second thought? What will be the center of your attention today? It is a never-ending struggle to discover inner focus techniques. Begin someplace. Begin small. Many of these exercises may seem strange at first, but harmful habits will be eliminated with continuous practice. Please let me know how you get on with these workouts later.

2.3 Mindfulness and Meditation Exercises

A wide range of people can benefit from mindfulness. It is a simple technique that has tremendous effects on the brain and may improve people's quality of life, personality, and peacefulness. Consider participating in one of the activities listed here if you have not already. The activities help us become more aware of our bodies, thoughts, and selves throughout time.

1- The Observer Meditation

The Observing Meditation explores why it is beneficial to get out of our internal thinking and feeling, a key component of Psychotherapy, which emphasizes mindfulness. Adopting an Observer mindset might help us put some space between who we are and problematic areas of our lives that we may be over identifying.

Follow these instructions to get started with the exercise:

1. Get relaxed in a sitting position.

2. Allow yourself to become comfortable in your own body and thoughts.

3. Make an effort to let go of thoughts and free your mind of its regular concerns.

4. Pay close attention to the area you are seated in initially. As you sit, see yourself on the outside, as if you were an outsider.

5. Now, turn your focus inwards to your body. As you sit on the chair, try to feel your body.

6. As you stay in contact with the seat, try to imagine the things your skin is touching, changing your mind to any physical feelings you are having. As you become aware of each one, recognize its presence before allowing your attention to let go of it and simply repeat.

❖ Recognize any feelings that arise and make room for them in your brain. Then return your focus to your watching self—your feelings and ideas are still present, but you are distinct from them, witnessing them.

This exercise may be performed for as long as you choose, and there are several phases you can go through to assist you in practicing becoming a self-observer. It is a difficult practice to begin with, since we are prone to react to and over-identify with our sensations.

If you are having problems moving outside of your mind and body, consider practicing the Self-Compassion Pause first to help you relax. The purpose of invoking the Observation Self is to shift into a different mode that allows you to take a step back from yourself and your surroundings. At the same time, you are interacting with a deeper, more consistent self that is unaffected by changing feelings.

2- Five Senses Exercise

This activity is called "five senses," It teaches you how to practice mindfulness in almost any setting. All that is required is to observe anything with each of your five senses.

To exercise the Five Senses, go in this order:

o   Make a list of five objects you can see.

Take a look around you and pick five items that catch your eye. Choose anything you would typically overlook, such as a shadow or a little fissure in the pavement.

o   Pay attention to four things you can sense.

Bring your attention to four sensations you are having right now, such as the texture of your jeans, the feel of the air on your skin, or the smooth surface of a table you are resting your hands on.

o   Pay attention to three things you can hear.

Take a minute to listen and make a mental note of three things you hear the sounds. This may be a bird's chirping, the refrigerator's humming, or the faint noises of traffic on a nearby road.

o   Take note of two items that you can smell.

Bring your attention to odors that you normally ignore, whether they are pleasant or not. When you are outside, the air could bring a scent of pine trees or the fragrance of a fast-food restaurant next door.

o   Take note of anything you can taste.

Concentrate on one item you can taste right now. You can take a sip of anything, bite a stick of candy, eat anything, or simply open your lips to scan the air for a flavor.

This brief and simple practice will immediately get you into a focused mood. The five senses practice can assist you to bring consciousness to the present moment in a short time.

3- The 3-Step Mindfulness Exercise

If you are short on time, this Worksheet has another wonderful workout for you. There are simply three steps to this exercise:

- **Step 1:** get out of "auto-pilot" mode and become aware of what you are doing, thinking, and perceiving right now.

Take a moment to reflect and adopt a relaxed yet dignified stance. Recognize and accept your feelings as they arise, but then let them go. Pay attention to who you are and where you are right now.

- **Step 2**: Focus on your breathing for six breaths or one minute.

The idea is to concentrate on one thing at a time: you are breathing. Be conscious of how your heart rises and lowers with each breath, as well as how your stomach pushes in and out and how your organs expand and contract. Find the rhythm of your breath and use it to bring yourself back to the present moment.

- **Step 3:** Expand consciousness outward, first with the body and then moving on to the surroundings.

Allow your attention to spread throughout your entire body. Take note of any feelings you are having, such as tightness, pains, or heaviness in your face or neck. Keep your body in thought as a whole, as a full container for your inner self. If you desire, you may widen your awareness to include the environment. Pay attention to what is right in front of you. Take note of the colors, forms, patterns, and textures of the items in front of you. Be mindful of your surroundings and present in this time.

When you are through the practice, slowly open your eyes and attempt to keep that attentiveness with you throughout the day.

4- The 3-Minute Breathing Space

Unlike meditations or body scans, this activity is simple and can help you start a mindfulness practice.

Thoughts typically arise during meditations and the body scan, making it difficult to maintain a calm and clear mind. This 3-Minute Breathing Space practice may be the ideal solution for people with hectic lives and brains. The workout is divided into three sections, each lasting one minute:

> ➢ The very first minute is spent trying to offer words and sentences to the inquiry "How am I doing right now?" while concentrating on the feelings, ideas, and emotions that come.

> ➢ The second minute is dedicated to maintaining breathing awareness.

> ➢ The final minute is intended to expand your focus outward from the breath, noticing how your breathing impacts the entire body.

Keeping a clear mind can be difficult, and ideas will inevitably arise. It is not so much about rejecting them as it is about allowing them to enter and then leave your head. Just keep an eye on them.

5- Observe a Leaf for Five Minutes

All you need for this activity is a leaf and your complete attention.

- Grab a leaf, carry it in your palm for 4 minutes, and give it your complete attention.
- Take note of the colors, shapes, textures, and patterns.

This will pull you into the present moment and match your thoughts with what you are going through right now.

6- Mindful Eating for Four Minutes

This practice requires conscious eating. Pay close attention to what you are holding and how it feels in your hands. Bring your attention to the scent after you have noted the texture, shape, color, and so on.

Finally, begin eating, but do it carefully and with complete concentration. Take note of the flavor and how it feels on your tongue. This activity may assist you in discovering new ways to enjoy familiar meals.

7- Observe Your Thoughts for 15 Minutes

This mindfulness practice is meant to increase your own attention simply.

- o To start, sit or lie down in a comfortable posture and try to relax all of your muscles.

- o Initially, concentrate on your breathing, then shift your attention to how you feel in your mind, and ultimately, to your emotions.

- o Recognize what comes into your mind, but control the desire to categorize or criticize it. Consider them as a fleeting cloud in your mental sky.

If your mind wanders away from your ideas, identify whatever it was that drew your attention away from your thoughts and gently redirect it back to your thinking.

8- Stare at the Center

The idea is to concentrate your attention on the center of the shifting color pattern. You may let your mind roam freely, observing whatever thoughts arise while remaining in the present moment.

This is analogous to the well-known calm fixation phenomena when looking at a burning candle or a bonfire.

This practice can help you focus and think deeply, but be cautious not to become lost in your ideas; rather, stay present at the moment and let the emotions pass you by.

9- Watch your movie

Imagine you are watching a movie, so you have to tell someone else whatever is going on. You must pay close attention and communicate clearly so that the other person understands what is going on.

That is the aim of this exercise. The only difference is that the picture is your life, and you are telling it to yourself rather than to someone else.

- o When you are ready, begin by concentrating on what you are doing and describing everything that is happening.
- o Be precise, detail-oriented, and straightforward.

You are attempting to raise awareness of how you are going about your business. We live on autopilot the majority of the time. This practice will help you become more conscious of your actions, regardless of how minor or small the activity at hand is.

10- The Body Scan

This is a well-known mindfulness activity. It is also a beginner's favorite. Pain is a sign; where and why are you experiencing it? Your body records everything that occurs to you. Muscle knots occur when our minds are also tense.

This exercise should be done many times each day. Every idle minute is a good chance to perform a body scan, whether it is cleaning your teeth, waiting at a bus stop, or in an escalator.

- ➢ Overcome the urge to pick up your phone — which we all do when we are in a hurry — and concentrate on your body instead.
- ➢ Take a deep breath and hold it for a few moments.
- ➢ Examine your hair, cheeks, throat, chest, stomach, legs, and limbs for any unusual behavior.

> Concentrate your breathing on the uncomfortable area; oxygen will help you relax.

11- Observe with your eyes closed

We are mostly distracted by our eyes, which move from one item to another and cause us to lose focus. Stopping noticing a distraction is sometimes the best way to eradicate it. This is a great exercise to do in a public place.

- Close your eyes for a moment.

- Relax by taking a big breath.

- Pay attention to what's going on out there you.

- Pay attention to things that are nearer to you first.

- Gradually begin to concentrate on the noises that are further away.

- Pay attention to what is happening directly next to you now.

- What are the sounds you are hearing? Are you able to hear voices? So, what exactly are they talking about?

- Continue the procedure with the sounds, noises, and voices further away.

Remember that you are attempting to comprehend rather than analyzing what's going on.

12- The Tangerine Experience

This practice is designed to help us improve our concentration on little details. You may also do this with a tomato, olive, or any other item you choose. Tangerines are my favorite fruits because of their unusual form and feel.

o   Take a close look at the food.

- Pay attention to the form of the thing.
- Put your hand on it and experience how it feels.
- Have fun with it.
- Examine how the form and texture respond to your body movement.
- Enjoy the smell of the fruit.
- Now keep your eyes closed and inhale deeply.
- For a moment or two, catch your breath and notice how long the smell lasts.

You may practice paying more attention by concentrating on just one fruit. When you focus on one thing, everything else vanishes.

2.4 Grounding Technique

According to Dr. Sara Allen, a psychotherapist, Grounding is an effective method for growing self-awareness and calming down rapidly. To assist us in returning to the present moment, we practice grounding activities. These strategies may be applied in various scenarios, such as when we are feeling "spacey," nervous, or stressed. When we are diverted by unwanted or upsetting ideas, memories, or urges, they can be utilized likewise if we deal with challenging or intense emotions such as rage, embarrassment, or despair. These may be used anywhere, at any time, to bring you back to the present, when situations are more controllable and pleasant than they are in our heads where we are anxious. Grounding activities are designed to help us become more conscious of the present moment's stability and inspire our bodies and minds to interact and collaborate. Allow yourself some time to think about some of the suggestions, and make some comments to come up with your own customized list.

1- Re-orienting yourself in the present

Answer the following questions to bring yourself back to the present time and place:

- o What is my age?
- o What is the date today?
- o Which year is coming up next?
- o What season is it?
- o Is it Wednesday or Friday?
- o What is this place around me?
- o Which month is going on?

Next, look around you for an object. Pay close attention to the object's form, color, texture, and functionality. Slowly shift your attention to a different thing and repeat. Then there's one more.

- o As you go through this, what do you observe about your mind?
- o How do you feel about your physical appearance?

These may sound unusual questions to ask yourself if you are feeling relatively calm as you read this. Still, it may be a really powerful approach to pull yourself back into the present moment when you are overwhelmed by emotions.

2- Using Your Senses to Get Grounded

Focus on each of your senses and write down one object you could see, feel, smell, hear, or touch right now.

- Remove your socks and shoes and pick a spot of ground to sit on.
- Try walking around and notice how the soil feels on your toes.

- Take a bath and pay attention to the water as it runs over your skin.

- If that is not an option, wash your face or run warm and cool water over your fingers.

- Take a moment to listen to the noises around you.

- Pay attention to the sounds you may hear around you.

- Pay attention to both subtle and more prominent noises.

- Then gradually broaden your attention outwards until you are concentrating on distant noises.

- Try to concentrate on both the less evident and the more dominating noises you can hear.

- Smell the fragrance of your favorite perfume, cologne, or essential oil.

- Make an effort to eat mindfully.

- Take something simple, like a fruit or vegetable or chocolates, and eat it slowly and thoughtfully, noticing the flavor and texture.

- Treat yourself to a self-massage.

To assist you in getting back into your body, begin on your toes and work your way up.

3- Imagining Yourself Somewhere Safe

Consider yourself in a secure, relaxing, pleasant, and peaceful environment. This place might be an actual or imaginary location where you feel completely comfortable.

Imagine this location in as much detail as possible, i.e.,

- How does it appear?
- What's going on around you?
- Can you tell me what it smells like?

- o Can you hear what's going on around you?
- o How hot is it outside?
- o Can you feel the breeze on your body?
- o Do you like to sit, jog, or walk?

Take note of how it feels to be fully calm and tranquil in this location.

- o What happens to your body and mind when you picture yourself in this location?

You might want to give this location a title or take note of it so you can return to it at any moment.

4- Grounding Through Movement

Take a long walk around the neighborhood or via a park. Paying attention to how your body moves. As you step, you can feel your feet moving, your toes touching the floor, and your arms going past your chest.

- As you move, what else do you notice in your body?
- Visit the gymnasium, go swimming, or schedule a yoga class.
- Do some jumping jacks.
- Pay attention to the sound and sensation of your feet making contact with the ground.
- Put on some songs and get your body moving. Have a dance if it seems right!

5- 54321

Look around you, wherever you are seated.

- Look for five items you can see in the area surrounding you.

- Look for four things that you may feel on your skin.

- Find three things you can hear.

- Look for two things that you can smell sitting there.

- Find one item you can taste with your mouth.

6- Touch and Describe

Pick up anything that you come across. Begin to explain it in your thoughts as if you were speaking to someone who has never seen something like it before.

o How would you characterize the material, size, color, and other distinguishing characteristics that someone else might picture it?

Continue to concentrate on the object's features and subtle qualities until the anxiousness subsides naturally.

7- Take a Short Walk

You can even measure your steps if you focus on them. Take note of the pattern of your movements and how it feels to press and then raise your foot.

8- Play a Memory Game

For ten seconds, look at a detailed image or photograph (such as a cityscape or other "dense" picture). Then, flip the photograph over and over in your head, trying to replicate it in as much info as possible. You can also make a mental note of everything you recall from the image.

9- Make Yourself Laugh

Make a ridiculous joke as you would see on a candy box or a popsicle stick. You may also get yourself a smile by viewing a humorous animal clip, a video from a performer or Television program you like, or anything else that makes you laugh.

10- Listen to Music

Play your favorite music as if it were the first time you have heard it. Pay attention to the tune and words.

- o Does the music give you the thrills or make you feel anything else?

Pay special attention to the sections that stimulate your interest.

➢ The cornerstone to all grounding strategies is to keep your attention on the current moment. This helps focus attention on the present moment and de-escalate worry and tension. When you are pressured or swamped with worrying feelings, the toughest part is continuing to use the techniques. Keep in mind that the more you practice these abilities daily, the more likely you are to execute them in high-stress circumstances when you need them the most.

2.5 Self-Awareness Training Activities

Self-awareness is essential for professional success. You can effectively direct the track of your life once you are self-aware. When you are self-aware, you can select where to concentrate your feelings, energies, and character. Self-awareness allows you to be more conscious of your ideas and feelings and how they influence your life. Learning to look at oneself objectively and attempting to view yourself as others see or interpret you is the greatest method to build self-awareness. The more self-aware you are, the easier it will be to improve and modify your life.

1- Self-Awareness Questions on Values and Life Goals

- o How is your ideal "you" in your mind?
- o What are your aspirations and visions?
- o What is the significance of these desires or goals?

- What is preventing you from achieving your aspirations or goals?

In your work, home, relations and affection, wealth, and other areas of your life, rank 5-10 of the most significant items in your life.

Now consider how much time you devote to each of these activities.

- What would you advise your kids to do or avoid doing?

2- Self-Awareness Questions on Personality

- Define yourself in three terms.
- Consider whether your behavior has changed since you were a youngster.
- Do you have either of your parents' personalities?
- What attributes in yourself do you appreciate the most?
- What is your greatest flaw?
- What is your greatest asset?
- What scares you the most?
- Do you make decisions based on logic or intuition?
- How would you respond to the hypothetical question "If?"

3- Self-Awareness Questions on Relationships

- Describe the kind of intimate connection you would like to have.
- Do you feel satisfied in your present relationship?

- ○ Who would you contact if you just had a few seconds to spend? What are your thoughts on the subject?

- ○ Which of your loved ones have you cherished the most?

- ○ Describe the finest moment in each of your relationships.

- ○ Define a relationship that has been shattered.

- ○ Examine if you handle yourself differently than others.

- ❖ The purpose of these questions is to get you to reflect. Answering these questions is a great way to learn more about yourself.

4- The Self-Awareness Worksheet

It has sets of questions that might assist a person in developing self-advocacy skills. This worksheet may be performed with the kids to help them become more aware of their strengths and shortcomings.

- ✛ I excel in the following areas:

- ✛ I'm having trouble with:

- ✛ The following are some of my favorite aspects of school:

- ✛ Here's how the teachers with whom I am most familiar manage this:

- ✛ The most challenging portion of my school day is:

- ✛ I would want some assistance with:

- ✛ When I need assistance, I am not afraid to ask for it in the following ways:

2.6 The Trigger Worksheet

The Triggers Worksheet is an excellent tool for learning more about what sets you off. Becoming aware of triggers may help you deal better in life. It can also benefit people suffering from anxiety, despair, anger control, and other disorders such as substance misuse.

The worksheet will assist you in identifying three triggers. After that, you will be asked to consider certain triggers by answering these questions:

- o What makes you feel this way?

- o How do you behave when you are triggered?

- o What would you need to remind yourself to stay in command when this trigger appears?

These questions can aid in the development of self-awareness and the strengthening of defensive mechanisms against negative beliefs, emotions, and actions.

1- The Setting of Life Goals Worksheet

This is another tool that can assist someone figure out what they want out of existence. This sort of tool may also inspire someone who is having difficulties in life. Goal-setting can help someone become more self-aware as they understand what it will take to reach their goals.

After identifying a goal, individuals are asked to elaborate on it by answering a set of questions such as:

- o What would you need to learn to attain this life's ambition?

- o What characteristics do you have that can assist you?

- o What difficulties do you expect to face?

- o Do you have a reliable support system in place?

- What motivates you to reach this goal?
- How would reaching this objective make you feel more fulfilled or happy?

2.7 Discovering Talent Worksheets

Once you have a sense of purpose, you understand how to implement your skills to make a difference in the world. Look for the connection of what you are great at, what you like to do the most, and what the world needs from your hidden skills.

Peer-to-Peer Interview Worksheet

The assessment of a person's interests, skills, and abilities, often known as sparks, is the cornerstone of this activity.

Six easy questions are included in the worksheet to assist someone in delving further into these concepts.

- What are some of your hobbies, skills, or abilities?
- How did you realize this was one of your sparks?
- What are your feelings like when you are getting your spark?
- Consider someone who is completely devoted to their spark/passion. Describe your observations.
- Do you have a spark supporter (a caring adult who assists you in exploring and honing your self-awareness abilities)? If you have answered yes, explain how this individual assists you.
- Do you have objectives and strategies in place to improve your spark/talent? If so, please provide an example.

Chapter 3: Emotional Regulation in DBT

Threats and rewards are expressed through emotions. Emotions can lead us to the appropriate actions, just like a compass does. Emotion control is one of Dialectical Behavior Therapy's key skill components. The emotional regulation section refers to the skills valuable to everyone who feels emotions (i.e., all of us!). However, they are incredibly useful to individuals suffering from mood or personality disorders, particularly those who have a borderline personality disorder (BPD). Individuals learn how to understand and embrace their feelings and also how to diminish their emotional fragility and instability, as well as their emotional pain, in this section.

For instance, when a kid makes a mistake, he may get afraid and lie to their family about it, or they may avoid facing them for fear of being punished. Their people would find out what they did ultimately, and the kid will certainly face the exact penalties that he was attempting to escape. In this case, the child's attempts to listen to and react to the 'fear' feeling were useless. However, someone being hunted by a dangerous animal in the woods would benefit from the same feeling (fear). It would have been wiser to flee rather than engage the dangerous beast in such a scenario. It is necessary to know when to trust emotional triggers and react to them and when not to. In other terms, we need to know how to control or manage our emotions to make the most use of them.

Understanding that unpleasant or painful emotions are not fundamentally harmful is one of the most crucial parts of therapy. Individuals are urged to acknowledge that no matter how joyful or well-balanced they are; they will surely encounter unpleasant emotions in their lives.

DBT clients gain crucial skills to keep their emotions in control and minimize emotional dysregulation, rather than focusing on avoiding or rejecting the presence of the unpleasant. In this chapter, I will go through the psychology of emotional regulation, including what it is, how to nurture it, and how to use emotional regulation in everyday life.

3.1 Emotion Regulation Strategies and Techniques

DBT's emphasis on actual, real-world strategies and skills is also one of the biggest strengths. You will not have to worry about abstract concepts about recovering and going forward in this type of treatment. Instead, the therapist will have a precise list of skills, tactics, and procedures that you can apply to start feeling and performing better. Below, I will share some emotional regulation secrets with you.

- **Understanding and Labelling Emotions**

Simply identifying and describing the emotion you are experiencing is one of the most important techniques in emotion management. Rather than using vague or generic phrases, DBT urges clients to utilize detailed descriptions of their feelings. This skill is based on the premise that you must first understand it to regulate emotion.

DBT individuals will also be able to understand the distinction between primary and secondary emotions and how to treat each most effectively.

Primary emotions are the first feelings you have in response to a situation or a stimulus in your surroundings.

Secondary emotions are the feelings or thoughts you have in response to your primary emotions or ideas.

Primary emotions are sometimes entirely normal responses to events in our lives, such as sadness when a family member dies or anger when someone treats us badly. On the other hand, secondary emotions are more harmful and less under our control. We normally have greater control over how we react to the reality that we are sorry when someone passes.

Secondary emotions may lead to negative and inappropriate actions, so it is critical to learn to embrace your core emotion without criticizing yourself for feeling it.

Our emotions are individual, organic experiences that cannot be shaped to match preconceived notions of "normal life," and attempting to do so can be harmful. Emotions, in reality, are adaptive evolutionary features that evolved to help us perform properly by assisting us in communicating with others and warning us of items in our surroundings that are either good or potentially troublesome.

Learning to detect, comprehend, and classify emotions is an extremely important ability to have. It will help you manage your own emotions and make you realize and sympathize with others.

- **Mindfulness**

Mindfulness is defined as staying in the now rather than in the old days or tomorrow. Mindfulness training helps us become more conscious of our thinking patterns, feelings, and how our thoughts and emotions influence our reactions to situations.

Mindfulness abilities are divided into two categories: "What" and "How" abilities:

"What" abilities:

- o Pay attention
- o Explain
- o Take part

"How" abilities:

- o Non-judgmental manner
- o Mindfully
- o Effectively

- **Letting Go of Painful Emotions**

Coping Difficult Emotions Mastering to let go, maybe the most crucial emotion management skill, can be tough but is well worth the time and effort. When it comes to processing unpleasant emotions, humans tend to become stuck. Rather than just letting go, we frequently cling to things even harder, worrying over every detail of our emotionality and questioning why it is occurring to us.

It may seem counterintuitive, but admitting that we are experiencing feelings, we would rather not experience can be the first step toward letting them go. When we admit that we are struggling, we stop avoiding tough feelings and face them head-on—and when we do, we may discover that the beast we believed we have been facing is a smaller and manageable creature.

To improve your capacity to let go of unpleasant feelings, _follow these steps_:

1. Keep an eye on your sensations. Recognize it, take a step back, and untangle yourself from it; try to see your feeling as a wave that comes and goes. It may be beneficial to concentrate on a specific aspect of the emotion, such as how your body feels or a mental image of it.

2. Recognize that your feeling is not you. Your emotions are a part of who you are, but they are not all who you are. You are more than your feelings; you are a whole person.

3. You do not have to act on your emotions. Just because you feel something does not mean you have to react to it. All you need to do now maybe sit with your feelings. Acting to cover up can often enhance and deepen a feeling.

4. Exercise LOVING your feelings is a good idea. This is a challenging notion to grasp.

We can start to love (admit) our emotional responses in the same way that we can start to love (acknowledge) any other aspect of ourselves. We cannot alter certain things, such as our age, height, wrinkles, the birds that make a song early morning that wake people up, the climate, the dimensions of our feet, allergies, and so on.

Remember that acceptance (love) and appreciation are not the same things. You do not have to enjoy your freckles, but they are what they are, and you cannot alter that, so accepting or loving them will make you feel so much better than resisting the fact that they exist.

- **Emotion Regulation Tips for the Holidays**

With the holidays approaching, you may be seeing family you do not see very often. These get-togethers may be fun ways to reconnect with friends and family, but they can also be hectic and emotionally challenging.

Get through your vacation trips with dignity and class, use these DBT self-help suggestions.

Take Good Care of Yourself

To begin with, it is incredibly beneficial to have a fit body to have a healthy mind. Eat nutritious foods, exercise frequently, get adequate sleep, avoid harmful or mood-altering drugs, and treat any diseases or conditions that require treatment. When we are sick, weary, or hungry, we do not make judgments, so addressing these bodily difficulties will help you keep your emotional equilibrium.

Boosting Positive Feelings

During the Holiday season, focus on strengthening your pleasant sentiments. You should not dismiss your unpleasant feelings, but you should also create a place for the good.

Look for ways to have a good time.

Allow yourself to appreciate yourself throughout the holidays by giving yourself freedom and the opportunity to do so.

Relationships should be worked on

Holiday get-togethers are an excellent occasion to mend and reestablish friendships with friends you have not seen in a long time. Allow yourself to be open to the possibilities of mending old connections and developing new ones. Most importantly, commit to preserving and enhancing your present connections with family, colleagues, and anybody else you will be seeing over your holiday travels.

Be aware of and conscious of the positive.

Focus on the positive aspects of your holiday season, such as visiting an old friend, receiving a very exciting gift, or attending a fantastic New Year's Evening party. Even if horrible things happen, there will always be one or two good things to enjoy.

Be unconcerned about your worries.

Concentrating on the good will make the following tip simpler to implement, putting your fears and anxieties aside. Replace all negative thoughts in your brain with all of the good ones you can think of. Remind yourself that you need to have fun, spend time with friends, and be surrounded by the love of your families. Make a place for the good in your thinking, and the bad will have less room to occupy.

3.2 Emotional Regulation Worksheets

Emotional management is vital for intellectual, interpersonal, and moral growth. Finding the perfect technique to teach emotional regulation to your children to help them cope with the unavoidable challenges of everyday life may be difficult for parents. Emotional perception and regulation are never the same for two individuals, which is why teaching someone to control their emotions may be challenging. However, psychologists have developed several excellent answers to this challenge throughout time.

- **Acceptance Worksheet**

This worksheet will assist you in identifying and comprehending a scenario or feeling that you are finding difficult to accept.

- o To begin, you must determine your circumstances: "What is the problem or situation?"

- o You then discuss the element of this circumstance that you find hardest to accept.

- o Then you go into detail about the facts of the problem.

- o Then you describe how you practice unconditional acceptance with your entire self (physically, emotionally, and spiritually).

The worksheet suggests the following activities:

"Take a deep breath and relax into an embracing, available spot. Become aware of any ideas or feelings that conflict with your truth, and then let them go. Use visualization, mindfulness exercises, or repetitions as acceptance approaches. Concentrate on a phrase of tolerance, such as "That's simply the way it is" or "Everything is as it should be."

Finally, on a scale from 0 to 10, evaluate your capacity to bear the discomfort of this challenging situation before and after practicing radical acceptance.

- **Interpersonal Skills Worksheet**

The DBT skills associated with interpersonal effectiveness, including objective efficiency, relational effectiveness, and personality effectiveness are listed in Interpersonal Skills Acronyms, along with helpful advice for putting these skills into practice.

The section on objective effectiveness abilities (DEAR MAN) provides an overview of each skill as well as advice for developing and using them:

Describe

To express whatever you want, use simple, specific phrases.

Don't mention, "Will you please wash?" Say something like, "Could you wash the dishes when you go to sleep?"

Express

Allow others to understand how you feel about a situation by expressing your emotions effectively.

Expect people not to be able to read your thinking.

Use the phrase "I felt because."

Assert

Do not hesitate; speak exactly what you need to convey.

Do not say, "Oh, well, I am not sure if I will be able to cook tomorrow or not".

Say, "I won't be capable of cooking since I'll be working late".

Reinforce

Reward those who respond well, and emphasize why you want a great conclusion.

A simple look and a "thank you" can be enough.

Mindful

Don't lose sight of the interaction's goal.

It is all too easy to get caught up in pointless debates and lose touch with your goals.

Appear

Make a confident impression.

Consider your nonverbal cues, stance, voice, and eye contact.

Negotiate

Nobody can always get all they desire out of their encounters.

Be willing to compromise.

"If you heat water, I'll cover them up," you can say.

- **Relationship Effectiveness Exercises**

The handout offers the following abilities under the Relational Effectiveness (GIVE) segment:

Gentle

During your encounters, do not criticize, harass, or pass judgment.

Accept "no" as a response to your demands on time.

Interested

Show that you care by paying attention to the other person without disrupting them.

Validate

Validate the other person's opinions and feelings on the outside.

Understand their emotions, recognize when your expectations are unreasonable, and respect their viewpoints.

Easy

Have a laid-back attitude.

Try to have a humorous demeanor and a smirk on your face.

- **Self-Respect Effectiveness**

Ultimately, in the Self-Respect Efficacy area, (FAST) skills are mentioned:

Fair

Don't only be fair towards others; be fair to yourself as well.

Apologies

If you make a request, have a viewpoint, or disagree, do not apologize until it is really necessary.

Set your values in mind

Speak up for what is right rather than compromising your beliefs to be accepted or acquire what you want.

Truthful

Overestimation, seeming helpless (as a sort of manipulation), and blatant lies are all examples of dishonesty.

When you are in a scenario where you are having trouble sticking to your standards, this handout may come in handy. The brief reminder and helpful recommendations might help you get back on schedule.

- **Action Tendency Worksheet**

This worksheet will assist you in increasing your understanding of action patterns that arise from both good and bad feelings.

The exercise will assist individuals in guiding through two key phases, each with a debrief.

Part One lets individuals understand how they react to emotions with a directed meditation. In a nutshell, you will:

o Invite someone to cover their eyes and think of a moment when they had to deal with difficult emotion. A dispute with a loved one is an instance. Urge them to visualize and relive the uncomfortable scenario as often as possible. What happened to them? Who were they hanging around with?

o Ask them to write down the strongest emotion or feeling that occurred from experience and try to locate it in their body if feasible. They should be able to name it ideally.

o Help them discover their natural reactions to the feeling. What do they want to do right now? It is important to note that this is not about how they responded at the time; rather what they wish to do now as they reflect on the event.

Part Two guides you through a meditation session similar to Part One, but this time they will focus on action inclinations associated with a good mood. This permits you and your clients to compare the two – what was unique about them? What did each of them observe about the other?

This Exploring Action Tendencies activity can assist your client in connecting the dots between a galvanizing event and their reaction to it. It can be very beneficial for individuals who want to address their compulsive tendencies or cravings, among other factors.

- **Emotional Regulation Skills Worksheet**

This is another useful handout for remembering the resources available to help you manage your emotions. The worksheet outlines four strategies you may use to enhance your emotion control and offers recommendations for putting them into practice.

Opposite Action

Opposite Action is the very first technique, and it may help you halt a strong or highly heated feeling in its path.

Emotions are frequently associated with certain behaviors; such as conflicts following rage or retreat following grief. However, we frequently think that the link is one of emotion to conduct rather than the other way along.

It is indeed feasible to elicit a feeling by participating in an action linked with that emotion rather than doing what you typically do when you are in a bad mood. If you are irritated, instead of screaming, try talking gently. If you are upset, instead of retreating from your pals, try conversing with them.

Check the Facts

It is all too simple to exaggerate things or place too much emphasis on your feelings.

This technique will assist you in recognizing this scenario as it occurs and then reducing the strength of the feelings.

To "verify the facts," ask the following questions:

- o What happened to make me feel this way?

- What preconceptions or perceptions do I have about the event?
- Does the strength of my feeling reflect the realities of the situation? Or does it simply confirm my presumptions about the situation?

P.L.E.A.S.E.

Another ability that recognizes the body-brain connection is the P.LE.A.S.E. skill. You will probably find it much simpler to control your emotions if you are also in control of your health and physique.

- PL – Treat Physical sickness
- E – Eat Healthy food
- A – Avoid Mood-Altering Medications
- S – Sleep Properly
- E – Exercising

Follow these tips to maintain your body in good shape, which will make it simpler to keep your mind in good shape.

Pay Attention to Positive Events

Individuals are surprisingly excellent at screening out the good and concentrating on the bad. It is normal, yet it is counterproductive!

Stop and reflect on the good if you discover you are focusing too much on the bad. You may practice by completing one tiny, positive activity each day and concentrating on the positive aspects as you go. Ignore little concerns and focus on joy, excitement, and satisfaction!

- Have a delicious, leisurely dinner
- Watch a film
- Connect with family or friends

- Find a local site such as a zoo or gallery
- Go for a stroll
- Put on earphones and do nothing but play music
- Have a lunch
- Give yourself a peaceful night in
- Try a new sport

- **The Emotion Regulation Questionnaire**

The Emotion Regulation Questionnaire (ERQ) is the most widely used emotion regulation measure among cognitive psychologists. It was created by James Gross and John Oliver in 2003, based on these five investigations that included question formulation, reliability, validity, and survey construction.

The scale consists of items assessed on a range of 1 (disagree strongly) to 7 (agree strongly), while four are neutral.

The following are the six components that make up the Cognitive Reappraisal aspect:

	Emotional Regulation Questionnaire	1	2	3	4	5	6	7
1	I change what I've been focusing on when I want to have a more favorable feeling (such as pleasure or humor)							
2	I change what I'm focusing on when I want to experience less unpleasant emotions (such as grief or rage)							
3	When I'm in a tense environment, I force myself to believe about it in a way that							

		1	2	3	4	5	6	7
	keeps me relaxed;							
4	When I want to experience more positivity, I transform the way I think about the scenario.							
5	I control my emotional responses by changing the way I believe about the scenario.							
6	When I want to feel less unpleasant feelings, I change how I believe about the circumstance.							

The four components of the Expressive Suppression facet are:

	Expressive Suppression facet	1	2	3	4	5	6	7
1	I keep my feelings to myself.							
2	While I am feeling happy, I try not to show it.							
3	I keep my emotions under control by not showing them.							
4	When I'm experiencing bad feelings, I try not to show them.							

- **Interpersonal Emotion Regulation Questionnaire**

The Interpersonal Emotional and Behavioral Questionnaire, or IERQ, was created to concentrate on emotional regulation processes instead of psychological interactions, which are less well-known.

It has 20 things and covers four variables, each with five items graded on a 5-point scale of 1 (not accurate for me at all) to 5 (true for me), where three is neutral.

The following are the four variables and their linked items:

	1- Enhancing Positive effect	1	2	3	4	5
1	I like to be around someone else when I am eager to share my happiness.					
2	Being in the existence of certain other individuals feels good when I am overjoyed.					
3	I like being in the existence of others when I am optimistic because it exaggerates the pleasant vibe.					
4	I strive out other people when I am pleased because pleasure is infectious.					
5	When I am overjoyed, I seek out other people to create them pleased.					

	2- Perspective Taking	1	2	3	4	5
1	When others notify me that things are not that bad as they appear, it tends to help me negotiate with my negative state.					

2	When I'm frustrated, everyone else makes me feel better by reminding me that things could be a lot nastier.					
3	When I'm agitated, others make me feel stronger by reminding me that things could be a lot severe.					
4	When I'm angry, others make me feel good by reminding me that it could be so much terrible.					
5	Others can make me feel better by telling me not to worry while I'm irritated.					
6	When I'm nervous, having someone tell me not to worry can help me relax.					

	3- Soothing	1	2	3	4	5
1	When I'm sad, I search for other people to sympathize with me.					
2	When I'm angry, I tend to seek out those who will sympathize with me.					
3	When I'm angry, I take refuge from people.					
4	When I'm depressed, I turn to other individuals only to know that I'm loved.					
5	When I'm upset, I look for anything to cheer me up.					

4- Social Modeling	1	2	3	4	5
1	Learning how others cope with their emotions helps me feel good.					
2	Hearing other person's opinions on how to manage problems helps me feel much better when I'm scared.					
3	Seeing how others might manage the same scenario helps me feel better when I'm irritated.					
4	It comforts me to hear what others have dealt with similar sentiments when I'm unhappy.					
5	When I'm unhappy, I prefer to think about what other people might do in my circumstance.					

This scale generates four scores, one for each subscale, computed by summing each item's score. The least amount of 5 and a maximum possible score of 25 are assigned to each subscale.

- **Cognitive Emotion Regulation Questionnaire**

The CERQ (Cognitive Emotion Regulation Question) is a tool for determining cognitive coping mechanisms employed after a bad event. It varies from previous emotional regulation surveys. It focuses on the individual's ideas rather than their conduct. It tries to learn about their thinking skills rather than how they act.

The scale consists of 36 items that are graded on a range of 1 (nearly never) to 5 (almost usually) ([almost] always). It has nine distinct cognitive coping techniques, each of which comprises four components.

Here are the nine strategies as well as an example item:

- *Self-blame* — I believe I am to blame for everything that has occurred.

- *Acceptance* - I believe I must accept that it has happened.

- *Rumination* – I am trying to figure out why I am feeling the way I am of what I have gone through.

- *Refocusing on the positive* — I imagine nice things that have nothing to do with it.

- *Refocus on Planning* - I consider how best to handle the problem.

- *Positive Reappraisal* - I believe that as a consequence of what has occurred, I can grow as a person;

- *Putting things in context* - I don't believe that it has been so horrible in comparison to other things.

- *Catastrophizing* - I frequently believe that what I have gone through is far worse than what others have gone through.

- *Other-blame* – I consider the errors done by others in this issue.

- **Emotional Regulation Through Pictures**

THE ZONES OF REGULATION

BLUE REST AREA	GREEN GO	YELLOW SLOW DOWN	RED STOP
SAD	HAPPY	NERVOUS	ANGRY
UPSET	EXCITED	SURPRISED	YELLING
HURT	CALM	CONFUSED	AGGRESSIVE
TIRED	PROUD	SILLY	MAD

Chapter 4: Ditch Stress for Good

It is easy to ignore the "ordinary" stress we experience from our jobs or schools, transportation, friendships, finances, and other factors in our daily lives. We keep going on "standby" until we are fatigued, worn out, and unhappy. So here, I am writing some stress coping techniques.

4.1 DBT Skills for Dealing Stress

Here are some DBT skills to relieve stress:

1. Mindfulness

Pay attention and keep an eye on things... What is your exact location?

Take note of your necessities.

Are you in touch with your Wise Mind (the crossroads of your rational and emotional minds)?

Rather than stressing about the previous or the next, bring yourself again into the present now.

2. STOP

- o **S**top,
- o **T**ake a deep breath and take a step back.
- o **O**bserve everything and take notes.
- o **P**roceed cautiously.

Before responding, take a moment and use Wise Mind to decide how to reply.

3. Pros and Cons

Are you unsure how to react in a certain situation?

Write out the advantages and disadvantages of using your abilities and being productive, as well as the advantages and disadvantages of acting impulsively or acting in the manner you would otherwise. This technique may incredibly be motivating and open your eyes to the potential immediate and long-term effects.

4. TIPP

- o   **T**emperature Adjustment
- o   **I**ntensive Activity
- o   **P**aced Breathe
- o   **P**airing Muscle Relief

These exercises will help you quickly modify your nerves and muscles and manage your emotions!

5. Radical Acceptance

Observe whether you are disputing or resisting reality. Even in the face of adversity, life may be worthwhile. By practicing *Half Smiling*, you may practice embracing your entire body.

4.2 Managing Stress Worksheets

Follow these exercises to relieve the stress disturbing your peace every moment.

1- Gratitude Exercises

Recognize the positive parts of your life no matter how small they are. Developing the habit of appreciation as a regular part of your day, may boost your pleasure, self-esteem, and overall health.

Gratitude Letter

Consider a person that you admire. This might be someone who has had a significant influence on your life or someone you would like to express gratitude to. Write a note to them expressing your gratitude, including detailed specifications and situations. It's entirely up to you whether or not you want to share the letter.

Gratitude Journal

Spend a couple of minutes every evening jotting down some positive aspects of your day. You could feel grateful for small things like a wonderful dinner, a conversation with a friend, or even a good night's sleep.

Grateful Contemplation

Eliminate all interruptions, including phones and television, and devote 5-10 minutes carefully assessing the problem. Consistency is key to this strategy. Consider it similar to brushing your teeth as your regular self-care routine. This strategy can be used in connection with meditation.

Mindfulness Walk

Take a stroll and make efforts to notice and enjoy your environment. You may achieve this by concentrating on each of your senses individually. Spend a minute simply listening, another minute just wandering around, and so on. Start to observe the sights, noises, scents, and feelings that you may otherwise overlook, such as a refreshing breeze.

Give Thanks

Keep your eyes alert during the day for opportunities to say "thank you," and make an effort to recognize them.

When someone goes out of their way to help you or others, tell the person that you appreciate what they have done and give a heartfelt "thank you".

Gratitude Conversation

Take turns sharing three things you were thankful for during the day with a friend. Take a moment to think about it. Rather than rushing through the list, spend time debating and pondering each item. Make this a regular part of your routine. By practicing before a meal, at sleep, or at some other normal time, you can develop a pattern.

2- Stress Exploration Worksheet

✓ *For each of the following areas, explain your major stresses and rank them on a scale of 1 to 10, with 1 being "a bit stressful" and 10 being "very stressful."*

Daily Hassles

Typical irritations or stresses in everyday life	
Examples: traffic, housework, work issues, insufficient sleep, schoolwork, limited spare time, and a disagreement with a spouse	
1	Ratings
2	
3	
4	

Healthy Coping Strategies

	Positive behaviors aid in reducing or managing stress and other unpleasant feelings. *Example*: Exercising, talking about difficulties, self-care, writing, and relaxation methods
1	
2	
3	
4	

Major Life Changes

	Important incidents, both good and bad that necessitate major change. *Example:* Child's birth, divorces, job offer, loss of a loved one, transfer, severe sickness or injury	
1		Ratings
2		

3		
4		

Life Circumstances

	Situations that make life difficult on a permanent and long basis. *Examples:* Unemployment or financial difficulties, handicap, chronic sickness, difficult partnerships, values at odds with society, racism, job unhappiness, and living in a hazardous environment	
1		Ratings
2		
3		
4		

Protective Factors

	Individual traits or living situations that help you avoid stress. *Example:* Financial security, excellent physical health, a loving family, a desire to succeed, and knowledge
1	
2	
3	
4	

Daily Uplifts

	Positive life events that bring you joy *Example:* Consuming a tasty meal, socializing with friends, engaging in recreational activities, and spending quality time in nature
1	

2	
3	
4	

3- Self-Care Worksheet

Self-care exercises help you check your fitness and well-being. Many of these tasks are likely to be something you currently undertake as part of your daily routine. This evaluation will ask you to consider how often and how well you perform various self-care exercises. The purpose of this assessment is to assist you in learning about your self-care requirements by identifying trends and areas in your lifestyle that require greater attention.

On this test, there are no perfect answers. There may be things that you do not want to participate in. This list is not extensive, but it might help you start thinking about your self-care requirements.

✓ *Select your answers as per the statements given below.*

1	I'm not very good at it	This is something I only do once in a while

2	This is something I can handle	This is something I do occasionally
3	This is something I excel at.	This is something I frequently do.
★	I'd like to get better at this	I'd like to do it more often

1	2	3	★	Physical Self-Care
				Take nutritious foods
				Maintain basic hygiene
				Rest when feeling sick
				Pay medical visits that are usually effective
				Get adequate rest
				Take part in enjoyable activities (dancing, singing, sports)
				Eat regularly
				Dress in a way that makes me feel good about myself
				Exercise
				Physical self-care in general

1	2	3	★	Psychological / Emotional Self-Care
				Make a soothing gesture (e.g., re-watch a favorite movie, hot bath)
				Going on outings with friends
				Recognize my talents and abilities
				I'm learning to express my emotions healthily (e.g., talking, writing a journal)
				Learn new skills that are not related to your job or education
				Disconnect yourself from any potential sources of distraction (e.g., phone, messaging)
				Take part in hobbies.
				Take a break from the job, study, and other commitments
				General emotional and psychological self-care

1	2	3	★	Social Self-Care
				Connect with older friends
				Spend some quality time with spouse
				Participate in fun activities with others
				Spend some time alone with family
				Make new friends
				Engage in interesting discussions
				Call or write to distant relatives and friends.
				I spend much time with people I admire
				Social self-care as a whole

4- Goal Breakdown Worksheet

Assume that you are looking for a new job. This is a significant task with a lot of phases that take time. Such a major aim might be difficult, if not downright overwhelming. This is the sort of goal you usually say that you will start "tomorrow" or "this week or next," but the week never seems to come because of laziness.

Breaking down your objectives into smaller tasks can help you avoid the stress and procrastination that comes with them. Finding new employment, for example, maybe broken down as follows:

Tips for Breaking Goals into Tasks

Unless essential, avoid setting projects that take more than an hour to complete.

A task may be too large if it's difficult to begin. Check to see if it can be divided up even more. "Play performing guitar," for instance, maybe broken down into "practice the start of a song."

Long activities that cannot be subdivided further should be given a time constraint (e.g., "Look at job postings for 30 minutes").

The tasks you set, do not have to be completed in a certain order. If a work proves to be more difficult than anticipated, break it down into smaller chunks or stretch it out over a longer period. Mix it with other activities if a task is simpler than planned.

Keep track of the time you set aside for activities. Turn off your cellphone, find somewhere quiet with minimal interruptions, and keep track of the time you have been doing with a schedule.

✓ *Here is a table for you to break your goals and schedule them.*

Goal Task	Required Time	Schedule Day
✦ .		
✦ .		
✦ .		
✦ .		
✦ .		
✦ .		
✦ .		
✦ .		
✦ .		

5- Healthy vs. Unhealthy Coping Strategies Worksheet

Coping techniques are behaviors we use to deal with stress, challenges, or unpleasant feelings, whether knowingly or unknowingly. Unhealthy coping mechanisms may feel wonderful in the short term, but they have detrimental long-term consequences. Healthy coping skills may not bring immediate gratification, but they result in long-term benefits.

✓ *Write your problems and the unhealthy coping strategies you used. Examples are given below.*

Examples of unhealthy coping strategies:	Examples of healthy coping strategies:
Taking Pain killers	Exercise
Sleeping deprivation	Seeking therapist help
Aggression	Mindfulness activities

Describe your problem briefly:

Unhealthy Coping Strategies	Consequences
↓ .	
↓ .	
↓ .	

6- Social Support Worksheet

Family, colleagues, organizations, and communities all give social support. This assistance can meet emotional, material, informational, or social requirements.

Benefits of Social Support

- A sense of safety
- Improved stress resistance
- Improvements in mental health
- Increased self-confidence
- More contentment in life
- Improved physical health

Building Social Support

Pay attention to the relationships you already have. Make contact with your friends and relatives. Maintaining your most critical connections should focus, even if other parts of your life are hectic.

Involve the community more. Take part in interest clubs, volunteer work, or religious organizations. This is a fantastic opportunity to meet new individuals who share your interests and establish a new support system.

Participate in support groups. Make friends with those going through similar issues or who have had comparable life experiences. Sharing your personal experiences and offering assistance to others may be a gratifying experience.

Make use of professional assistance. Doctors, psychologists, social services, and other specialists can assist you in resolving issues that are more complex or difficult to manage on your own.

✓ *Now think of your real supporters and write about them.*

	Your Social Supporters	How do they Help You?
#1		
#2		
#3		

Chapter 5: Facing Your Feelings: Distress Tolerance

The capacity to handle real or perceived emotional pain is referred to as distress tolerance. It also entails getting through an emotional ordeal without exacerbating the situation. People with poor distress tolerance are easily overwhelmed by tense events and resort to harmful or even destructive coping mechanisms to deal with their pain.

Throughout life, everyone encounters a range of stressors. These pressures can range from minor irritations to severe life events such as losing employment, separation, or a loved one's demise. Regardless of how severe the stress is, your ability to tolerate suffering can influence how you handle the circumstance. Mastering distress tolerance skills can significantly improve your ability to deal with tough emotions.

5.1 Distress Tolerance Skills

This information aims to give you some background on distress intolerance and suggestions for better managing stressful or uncomfortable emotions. This is broken down into modules that should be completed in order. Although it is not required, it is encouraged that you finish one module before moving on to the next. Information, exercises, and recommended activities or tasks are all included in these skills.

- **Accepting Distress**

Starting to perceive your emotions and feelings differently is the first step toward tolerating distress. Emotional distress is a relatively common occurrence in humans. Sadness, rage, and anxiety are all-natural reactions to being human. These feelings are not only common, natural, and acceptable; they are also important and beneficial to us. Accepting hardship does not imply that you must like emotional pain, that you must accept that you will be unhappy, or that you must wallow in unpleasant feelings. On the other hand, accepting distress is seeing the bad emotion for what it is and adjusting how you respond to it. Accepting your emotion and reacting to it positively can often change how it affects you.

Starting with being aware of your emotions when you are not upset is a smart technique to acquire the skill of accepting discomfort. This will offer you some practice with the skill of monitoring your emotions in less stressful situations (i.e., when you aren't upset), so you'll be better equipped to apply it in more difficult situations (i.e., when you are distressed). A short script runs across the page to assist you through the practice of being aware of your emotions at any moment.

Mindfulness of Emotion Diary

	Sunday	Monday	Tuesday	Wednesday	Thursday	Friday	Saturday
Time							
Duration							
Experience							

Guide: Grab a seat on the sofa that is most comfortable for you. Feet flat on the ground, arms at your sides, and a stool that fully supports your body. Close your eyes for a moment. Begin by focusing on your breathing and taking a few deep breaths to relax. Now softly direct your focus to how you are experiencing emotionally within yourself. Take note of any emotions in you, whether they are pleasant, negative, or sad. Whether they are intensely weak or strong. For the next 10 to 15 minutes, try maintaining your mindfulness practice.

- **Improving Distress**

Understanding and improving distress are two quite distinct approaches, and the key to developing distress tolerance is to strike a reasonable balance. Some people avoid distressing situations, participate in reassurance seeking or monitoring to relieve their distress or utilize distraction and repression to reduce their distress. Others numb and withdraw by abusing drinks or drugs, binge eating, or sleeping through their emotions. Others may indulge in harmful escapes, causing physical harm to themselves as a way of coping with their grief. Although these behaviors vary greatly, thus so do the solutions for alleviating distress. The general driving idea for alleviating distress is to perform the polar opposite of your escape impulse and identify specific activities that improve your psychological response.

Personalizing and clarifying ideas for your particular situation is beneficial. An example of a personalized list may be seen in the image below. Make your list now.

Improving Distress Diary	
What Not To Do	**What To Do**
Example: I try to avoid leaving the house since it makes me feel bad.	_Example_: I face my anxiety by getting out of the house, without earphones, and without depending on family for comfort.

- **Tolerating Distress**

By creating a unique Distress Tolerance Implementation Plan in the last module, you may tie all tactics together. The best ways to implement this plan regularly are addressed to improve emotional well-being. There are five main steps in the Distress Tolerance Plan of action:

- Understanding distress triggers
- Detecting distress warning signs
- Choosing to forgo escape methods in favor of the opposing action
- Accepting distress with the help of mindfulness techniques
- Distress reduction through distress improvement efforts

Identify your Distress Intolerant Beliefs and check these beliefs by answering the following questions.

If I'm in a state of emotional discomfort, then...

What is going to happen?

_____
_____
_____
_____

What is it going to be like?

_____
_____
_____
_____

What does this mean for me?

_____
_____
_____
_____

What I'll have to do?

_____
_____
_____
_____

Try to condense your responses into one main Distress Intolerant Thought you firmly hold.

Emotional pain is harmful because...

_____
_____

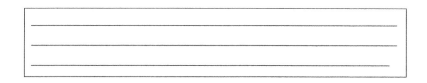

It is crucial to remember that if you stick to your Distress Tolerance Plan of action and face your distress instead of avoiding it, your pain intolerant attitudes will weaken and vary over time. This is because simply by accepting your distress, you will collect evidence and situations demonstrating that your beliefs are false.

5.2 Distress Tolerance Exercises and Worksheets

Now, I will mention some of the distress tolerance exercises and activities that can help you with your emotions.

- **Distracting Exercises**

With Activities

Tolerance makes you feel better, and as you start feeling better and more productive, endorphins are secreted, and your self-esteem grows. You can obtain a positive feeling from physical activity since chemicals are released when we push ourselves. Workout, interests, cleaning, going to community events, calling or visiting a friend, playing computer games, going for a walk, working, playing, participating in sports, going out to eat, drinking decaf tea or coffee, going fishing, chopping wood, gardening, or playing pinball are all examples of physical activities. Whatever fits for you is what you should do.

With Emotions

(Opposite Feelings): Make sure whatever you do, produces the polar opposite of the emotion you are experiencing. You might watch comedians as well as emotional movies. Read books or stories that will make you cry.

With Pushing Away

Move the problem away by ignoring it for a bit, and then mentally leave the environment. Create a mental barrier between yourself and the issue, or drive it away from your thoughts by filtering it out. Censor rethinking. Refuse to consider the negative sides of the situation. Place the pain on a rack. Put it in a box and store it for a while.

With Contributing

Provide help to anyone, volunteer, contribute to others, do something lovely for somebody, do something unexpected and considerate.

With Comparisons

Watch calamity movies, reality T.V shows, visit an Emergency or hospital waiting room, and compare yourself to those dealing similarly to you or less well.

With Thoughts

Count to ten; count the colors in a picture, a plant, or a view outside. Work on puzzles, watch Television and read.

With Sensations

Holding ice in your hand, squeezing a rubber ball firmly, taking a warm shower, listening to loud music, snapping an elastic band on your ankle, sucking on a lemon are some more strong experiences.

1- SELF SOOTHE

With Vision

Purchase one lovely flower, decorate one area of a room, light candles, and observe the flame. Make a lovely table with your best items for a meal. Visit a lovely art museum. Sit in a gorgeous old hotel hallway. Take a look around you at the natural world. Go outside late at night and gaze at the stars. Take a stroll in a lovely portion of town. Make sure your nails are in good shape. Look through a book for gorgeous photographs. Attend a ballet or other dancing event in person or on television. Avoid lingering on any of the sights that pass in front of you.

With Taste

Enjoy a delicious dinner and a soothing beverage, such as mint tea or hot cocoa (but no alcohol). Allow yourself to delight a dessert. Make your coffee with condensed milk. At an ice cream shop, try out different flavors. Suck on a peppermint candy chunk. Taste the meal you are eating, one bite at a time, concentrating on the flavor.

With Smell

Spray fragrances in the air, light a candle, or use your favorite perfume or cosmetics (or try them on at the store). Use lemon oil to freshen up your decor. In your bedroom, place potpourris in a vase. Bake biscuits, cake, or toast with spice. Take a deep breath and smell the roses. Take a walk in the woods and take in the fresh scents of nature.

With Hearing

Listen to lovely or relaxing music, or stimulating and exhilarating music, with your senses. Pay attention to natural sounds such as waves, animals, rain, and whispering leaves. Sing your favorite songs, hum a relaxing tune, or pick up a musical instrument. To hear a person's voice, dial 800 or other service numbers. Allow any noises that come your way to pass through one ear and out the other.

With Touch

Feel whatever you are touching and notice how peaceful it feels. Take a warm bath, change your bedding, cuddle your dog or cat, get a massage, soak your toes, and cover your entire body in thick lotion. Put an ice pack on your head, burrow into a plush chair at a hotel lobby or home, and dress in a silky top, frock, or scarf. Try on a pair of gloves with a fur lining. Brush your hair over an extended period.

2- Improve the Moment

With Imagery

Consider depictions of soldiers who fought and won in a peaceful environment. Consider how you may decorate a hidden space within yourself. When you feel intimidated, go to the bedroom. Anything that has the potential to harm you should be kept out. Assume everything goes according to plan. Consider how well you can cope. Make up a relaxing and attractive imagination world and let your mind wander there. Imagine your negative emotions draining like water from a pipe.

With Meaning

Find or construct some reason, purpose, or worth in bodily or mental pain (build a track record of perseverance). Spiritual ideals should be remembered, listened to, or read on. Concentrate on the good parts of a difficult circumstance that you can identify. In your thoughts, repeat them again and over.

With Relaxation

Find a sense of humor and smile. Start with your wrists and elbows and make your way up to the top of your head before releasing each muscular group. Take a hot shower or soak in a hot tub while listening to a relaxation disc. Drink warm milk, rub your shoulders and head or your calves and toes, and soak in a bathtub of very cold or very hot water for as long as you can stand it. Take deep breaths, give a half-smile, and change your face expressions.

With One Thing at a Time

Concentrate all of your focus on what you are accomplishing right now. Keep your focus on where you are in the current moment. Concentrate all of your attention on the body symptoms that come with nonjudgmental activities. (For example, walking, cleaning, dishwashing, scrubbing, and repairing). Keep track of how your body moves as you complete each task. Exercise your attentiveness.

With Prayer

(Walking and talking aloud, or kneeling and praying to your higher authority, God, Queen, or whoever) Whatever that means to you, tell your story to a superior being with great insight. For example, it could be Lord or your wise thinking. Invoke the strength to face the agony right now. Give all to God or a higher power.

With Vacation

Allow yourself a brief break. For example, get in bed between 3 to 4 p.m. and draw the blankets over your head for twenty minutes. For a day or more, get a motel room near the beach or in the mountains. Allow your answering service to monitor your calls or disconnect your phone for the day. Take a one-hour break from the work you need to get done. Look through a book, curl up in a chair, and bite gently. Take a rest from adulthood and allow yourself to be a child once more.

With Encouragement

Take charge of your happiness. Repeat this phrase again and over: "It's not too much for me. This is not going to last forever. I am going to make it work. I am doing everything I can. I am confident in my abilities. I am fine."

- **Observing Breath Exercises**

- Concentrate on your breath as it enters and exits your body.
- As a means to center yourself in your wise thought, pay attention to your breathing.
- Watch your breathing as a means of regaining control of your mind, letting go of non-acceptance, and resisting reality.

Deep Breathing

Lie down flat on your back. Put your attention on the motion of your tummy while you inhale evenly and softly. Allow your belly to rise as you breathe in, allowing air to enter the lower portion of your chest. As the upper halves of your respiratory tract begin to fill with air, your chest rises, and your stomach goes down. Do not get too tired. Continue for another ten breaths. The inhalation will be followed by an exhale lengthier than the intake.

Ten Breaths

Increase the length of your exhales by one footstep. Check to see if the inhalation elongates by one step as well. Only extend the inhale if you feel it will please you. Return your breathing to normal after Twenty breaths. After around five minutes, you can resume your practice of longer breaths. Return to normal as soon as you sense a slight bit of fatigue. After a few sessions of longer breath practice, your exhale and inhalation will be of similar duration.

Before getting back to normal, do not practice long, regular breaths for more than ten breaths.

By Footsteps

Keep walking in a yard, along a pavement, or on a path in a passageway. Take a normal breath. By counting your steps, you can determine the length of your breath, both exhale and inhalation. Keep going for a few moments. Start by increasing the length of your exhale by one step. Exhalation should not be forced. Allow nature to take its course. Keep a close eye on your inhalation to determine whether you want to lengthen it.

Listening to Music

Play a piece of music for yourself. Long, soft, and even breaths are recommended. Watch your breath and control it while staying conscious of the music's flow and moods. Strive to be a master of your breathing and yourself, rather than getting lost in the music.

Counting Your Breath

Lay cross-legged on the ground (if you understand how, sitting in the full or half-lotus posture) or sit at a desk with your feet on the ground, or bend or lie flat on the ground; or go for a walk.

- Be conscious that "I am inhaling" while you inhale.

- Be conscious that "I am exhaling" while you exhale.

- It is important to remember to inhale from your stomach.

- Remember that "I am inhaling" when you breathe the second inhale.

- As you slowly exhale, keep in mind that "I am exhaling."

- Continue to number 10 and beyond. Return to 1 once you have reached ten.

- Continue to 1 if you lose track.

Breath in a Conversation

Long, soft, and even breaths are recommended while hearing a friend's comments and responding to them. Keep your breath in check. Carry on with the songs.

Continuing The Breath

Lay cross-legged on the ground (if you understand how to sit in half or full lotus posture), sit at a desk with your feet on the ground, or go for a walk.

- Start inhaling slowly and naturally (from the abdomen), keeping in mind that "I am inhaling properly."

- "I am exhaling properly," exhale in mindfulness.

- Repeat for a total of three breaths.

- Extend the inhale on the fourth inhalation, noticing that "I am blowing out a long exhale."

- Repeat for a total of three breaths.

- Now pay close attention to your breathing, being aware of every movement of your abdomen and lungs. Follow the path of air as it enters and exits.

- "I am inhaling and tracking the inhale from start to finish," stay mindful.

- "I'm exhaling, and I'm watching the exhale from start to finish."

Repeat for a total of 20 breaths. Return to your previous state. Repeat these steps after 2 - 3 minutes.

While breathing, keep a half-smile on your face. Move on to the next practice once you have mastered this one.

The Mind and Body

Pose cross-legged on the ground (if you know it, sit in the full or half-lotus posture), sit upright with your feet on the ground, bend, or lie flat on the ground.

- Pay attention to your breathing. Continue to exhale and inhale very gently until your body and mind are calmed down.

- Keep in mind that "I'm taking a deep breath in and relaxing my body and mind. I'm inhaling and letting go of the tension in my body."

- Repeat for three more breaths, prompting the thought, "I'm taking a deep breath in a while; my mind and body are at ease. I'm exhaling when my body and mind are relaxed."

- Maintain awareness of this thought for 30 to 60 minutes, depending on your abilities and time available.

- The practice must be easy and mild at the start and end. When you are ready to quit, massage your thigh muscles gently before resuming your regular sitting posture.

- Before you stand up, take a moment to RELAX.

- **Half Smile Exercises**

With your emotions, face the realities of your life. Relax your facial, throat, and shoulder muscles (by releasing go or clenching and then releasing free) and half-smile with your lip. A grin is a strained smirk. A half-smile is defined by slightly tilted lips and a relaxed expression. Make an effort to maintain a calm attitude. Keep in mind that your body interacts with your thoughts.

During Free Moments

Half-smile wherever you find yourself seated or walking. Smile at a kid, a flower, a wall art, or anything else that is reasonably still. Three times silently inhale and exhale.

Listening to Music

For two or three minutes, listen to some music. Pay close attention to the music's words, melodies, tempo, and emotions. At the same time, keeping an eye on your breaths and breathing patterns, half-smile.

In the Morning

Hang a leaf, any other decoration, or even the phrase "smile" on the wall or ceiling so that when you open up your eyes, you see it immediately once. This sign will be displayed as a warning. Take a few seconds before getting out of bed to catch your breath. Take three gentle breaths in and out while keeping a half-smile. Keep track of your breaths.

In a Sitting Position

Sit on the floor with your spine straight or in a seat with both feet on the ground. Half-smile. Keep a half-smile while you take a breath.

When Irritated

Half-smile as soon as you realize, "I'm angry." For three breaths, silently inhale and exhale while keeping a half-smile.

Lying-Down Position

Lie down on a level surface without a cushion or mattress to assist you. Keep your arms at your sides and your legs slightly apart and extended out in front of you. Keep a half-smile on your face. Gently inhale and exhale, focusing your concentration on your breath. Allow every joint in your body to relax. Relax each muscle as if it were falling into the ground or as if it were as soft and pliable as a strand of silk drying in the breeze. Allow yourself to completely relax, focusing simply on your breathing and a half-smile.

The Hateful Situation

Take a seat calmly. Take a deep breath and give a half-smile. Take a mental picture of the individual who has brought you the most pain. Consider the characteristics you despise, dislike, or find the most disgusting. Examine what makes this person joyful and what makes them suffer in their daily lives. Consider the person's views; consider the person's thinking and reasoning tendencies. Investigate the motivations behind this person's hopes and deeds. Finally, assess the individual's level of awareness. Check if the person's perspectives and views are open and public and if they have been impacted by biases, narrow-mindedness, hostility, or rage. Check to see if the guy is in command of himself. Keep until you feel empathy flow up in your heart like a well of clean water, and your wrath and resentment go away. Repeat the exercise on the same person several times.

- **Awareness Exercises**

Making Tea or Coffee

Make a mug of tea or coffee to present as a welcome gift or to enjoy on your own. Slowly and deliberately perform each action. Do not let a single element of your motions pass you by unnoticed. You should be aware that your hand raises the mug by the grip. Be aware that you are preparing a cup of aromatic hot tea or coffee. Each step-in-awareness should be followed. Breathe more slowly and deeply than normal. If your mind wanders, take a deep breath and hold it.

Connection to the Universe

Pay attention to where your body makes contact with an item. Consider all of the ways you are linked to and welcomed by that item. Assess the object's purpose concerning you. Evaluate what the object can do for you. Consider its goodwill in doing so. Feel the sensation of holding the object and concentrate your complete attention on that act of kindness until you feel connected, cherished, or cared for.

Examples:

Concentrate on your feet as they touch the floor. Consider how the ground is friendly to you, supporting you up and offering a path to other things rather than letting you slip away from anything else.

Concentrate your attention on the part of your body that is in contact with the chair you are sitting in. Consider how the chair embraces you completely, keeps you up, protects your back, and prevents you from collapsing to the floor.

Pay special attention to your bed's sheets and blankets. Consider the feel of the sheets and blankets around you, holding you in place and making you warm and comfy.

Take a look at the room's decor. They provide protection from the wind, the heat, and the snow. Consider how the ground and the air in the area link the walls to you. Feel your relationship to the walls that give you a safe environment to accomplish your work.

Give a plant an embrace. Consider how you and the plant are linked. You and the plant both have life, and you are both heated by the sunlight, held by the air, and sustained by the land. Try to imagine the plant caring for you by giving you something to rely on or shade you.

Positions of the Body

This can be done at any time and location. Begin to concentrate on your breathing. Breathe more slowly and deeply than usual. Always be aware of your body's posture, whether you are walking, sitting, lying on the ground, or resting.

Know where you are walking, standing, lying, or sitting. Keep in mind what your job requires. For instance, you may be aware that you are standing on a grassy hillside to replenish yourself, practice breathing, or simply stand. Be conscious that if you do not have a purpose and direction, you cannot be aware.

Washing The Dishes

Wash the dishes slowly and deliberately, as though each dish is a work of art. Each dish should be treated with care. To keep your attention from wandering, focus on your breathing. Do not try to rush through the process. Consider dishwashing to be the most important task in your life.

Hand-Washing Clothes

Washing too much clothing at once is not a good idea. Choose no more than three or four pieces of apparel. To avoid pain, find the most comfortable posture. Deliberately scrub the clothing. Keep your focus on your arms and hands at all times. Keep an eye on the water and soap. Your body and mind will seem as nice and clean as your clothes once you have finished cleaning and washing. Remember to keep a half-smile on your face when you have lots of thoughts in your mind and take a deep breath.

Taking A Bath

To take a shower, set about 45 minutes. Do not even think of hurrying. Allow every movement to be soft and deliberate, from when you pour the bathwater until you put on fresh clothes. While putting on clean clothes, pay attention to every detail and keep your movements light and quiet. Keep your eyes alert for any movement. Without judgment or fear, pay attention to every aspect of your body. Keep an eye on each drop of water that reaches your body. Your mind will seem as serene and weightless as your body once you have finished. Pay attention to your breathing. Consider yourself in a summertime lotus pond, which is clean and aromatic.

Practicing Meditation

Relax with your backstretch on the floor or in a seat with both feet on the ground. Close your eyes completely or partially open them and look at something nearby. Mention the word "ONE" to yourself calmly and softly with each inhalation. Say the word "ONE" as you breathe. Say the word "ONE" softly and quietly as you exhale. Try to condense your entire mind into just one word. When your mind wanders, gently bring it back to "ONE."

If you feel the urge to move, resist it. Simply monitor your desire to move. Continue to practice a little past the point where you wish to stop. Simply watch your desire to stop.

Cleaning The House

In phases, sorting things out and putting things away, cleaning the toilet, scouring the restroom, sweeping floors, and dusting should be done. Allow sufficient time for each task. Slowly walk, three times slower than normal. Concentrate your entire attention on each activity. Take a glance at the novel, be conscious of what it is, understand that you are in the way of placing it on the bookshelf, and understand that you aim to put it in that exact location while placing it on the rack, for instance. Know that your arm seeks for and takes up the book. Any movement that is abrupt or rough should be avoided. Keep your focus on your breathing, especially when your mind wanders.

Scenario One

When you arrive at work, your supervisor notices that you are half an hour late. What will your emotions be like? What DBT strategies can you employ to assist you in managing your feelings and the conflict?

Scenario Two

You are in a family scenario, and everyone is telling you that you need to find employment and that you did not get one because of your laziness. What will your emotions be like? What DBT strategies can you employ to assist you in managing your feelings and the conflict?

Scenario Three

You are in a great mood and want to go shopping, but your friends refuse to accompany you. What will your emotions be like? What DBT strategies can you employ to assist you in managing your emotions and the conflict?

Scenario Four

You are in the physician's surgery, and she refuses to give sleeping medication because she fears you will overdo it? What will your emotions be like? What DBT strategies can you employ to assist you in managing your emotions and the conflict?

- **Basic Principles of Accepting Reality Worksheet**

Dealing with reality does not imply that you must like the situation. Breathing, a half-smile, and consciousness are some tools that can help you accept the truth. Radical Acceptance, for instance: I have suicidal ideas all of the time, but that doesn't indicate I like them or will execute them.

Turning The Mind

Acceptance of truth necessitates a decision. It is as though you have arrived at a crossroads. You must direct your thoughts away from the path of denial and onto the path of acceptance. To accept, you must make an inner Devotion. Acceptance is not the same as willingness to accept. It simply directs your attention to the way. It is, however, the first stage. You must repeat the process of turning your thoughts and committing to acceptance. You may be required to commit several times in the period of a few moments.

Willfulness

When action is required, willfulness is like resting on your arms and failing to make the necessary changes. Willfulness creates you to resist any recommendations that would alleviate your distress and make it more bearable.

Giving up is a form of willfulness. It is the polar opposite of doing what is productive. Willfulness entails rectifying every circumstance or refusing to accept the unpleasant situation.

Willingness

Develop a WILLING reaction to each scenario. Willingness is doing exactly what is required in each scenario in a non-obtrusive manner. It concentrates on efficiency. Willingness involves paying close attention to your WISE BRAIN and acting by your inner self. Willingness means recognizing your relationship to the universe, including the planet, the floor you are standing on, the chair you are sitting in, and the person you are speaking with. Consider whether the situation that is causing the distress is critical.

Radical Acceptance

It is letting yourself entirely surrender to whatever situation you are in. Allow yourself to let go of the need to battle reality.

The Only Way Out

- Pain only causes misery when you fail to admit it.

- ACCEPTANCE means deciding to put up with the situation for the time being.

- ACCEPTANCE entails admitting what already exists.

- Accepting things is not the same as approving them.

As long as you acknowledge your illness or your inaccurate views of events or social communication challenges, the fury or anger you experience will subside if you quit resisting. When you are ready to accept, you will be shocked at how lighter you will feel.

- **Distress Tolerance Coloring Charts**

Chapter 6: Interpersonal Effectiveness

By completing the mindfulness and emotion regulation training course in dialectical behavior therapy (DBT), readers can go to the next core skills component and interpersonal effectiveness. These abilities are crucial because how we interact with people greatly influences the quality of our connections and how our interactions turn out. DBT participants are given strategies to help them approach discussions more carefully rather than behaving and responding impulsively due to stress or powerful emotions to interact more efficiently. The capacity to ask for something and, when necessary, say no to the requests are two crucial components of interpersonal effectiveness.

6.1 Interpersonal Skills Development

A relationship can be compared to a large, leafy tree. A strong root system is required to sustain and support a tree. The tree becomes bigger, harder, and more established as the roots grow and may even blossom. Your interpersonal connections, like the tree, possess roots. Good roots are necessary for the growth of a healthy relationship. DBT (Dialectical Behavioral Therapy) teaches specialized strategies for establishing deep roots and maintaining healthy relationships.

The interpersonal effectiveness skills taught in DBT are designed to help people form and sustain meaningful connections. People who have had a lot of positive relationships throughout their life are more likely to have these talents. These characteristics have been analyzed by DBT and turned into practical abilities. These abilities may be beneficial for anybody, but they are especially beneficial for those who have suffered from trauma or an emotional problem.

- **THINK**

THINK is a DBT interaction effectiveness skill that is relatively new. It was created to help people deal with their unpleasant feelings against others. You do not need to utilize this talent in every conversation, but it will be helpful while dealing with interpersonal issues and frustrations.

- **Think** about the problem from the other person's point of view. Is she angry as well? Does she also see you as ridiculous, just as you are seeing her to be unreasonable?

- **Have Empathy** - Can you imagine what it is like to be the other person? Allow yourself to be moved by her feelings for a minute.

- **Interpretations** – of the actions of others. Consider the reasons why she did the action that bothered you. Begin with irrational reasons (to broaden your mind) and work your way down to more practical ones.

  Take note of the other people. Pay attention when she attempts to be kind to improve the friendship. Even though you believed she was upset, she seemed to be terrified. Even if you are not on speaking terms, notice how she looked at you. You do not have to do something about it right now; keep an eye on it.

- **Kindness** – in the way you responded. This does not imply that you must forgive and forget right away. Simply said, this signifies that your thoughts are kind. You may respond, "What you just said to me was upsetting, and I hope we can work this out in the future". I'm in serious need of some space right now." A thoughtful answer is preferable to name-calling and shouting.

- **Boundary Building Skill**

The boundary building skill is linked to our emotional well-being. Learning to utilize boundaries is among the most difficult sets of clothes to put on when we grow up in a poor or unstable home. As a result, it runs against every strand (or cell) of our nature. We begin to regard ourselves as distinct from others. It feels great to have clear and intact limits. We may select what to let in and stay out within healthy limits because they are flexible. We may choose to let compassion, kindness, and good esteem in a while excluding meanness and hatred.

6.2 Interpersonal Skills Worksheets

Irrespective of how the client values objectives, relationships, and self-respect efficiency for that particular engagement, the interpersonal skills learned in DBT can raise the chances of good results. When implemented properly, the abilities enable an individual to properly communicate their wants and desires without the need for the opposing party to "read their thoughts." It allows a person to ask for whatever they want courteously and honestly while still considering the other person's sentiments and maintaining the relationship.

- **Skills Assessment Activity**

What is the most crucial ability a person may obtain?

Several skills may be added to, increased, and excelled on. Thousands of programs, billions of articles and books, countless suggestions and recommendations are available to help us enhance our lives by mastering a certain skill or group of talents.

But which is the most crucial?

There is not a clear answer to that issue, but I believe you will obtain the best response by doing this activity.

1	Very poor
2	Poor
3	Sometimes good
4	Usually, good
5	Always good

	✓ Give yourself a score on the following abilities.	1	2	3	4	5
1.	Introducing yourself					
2.	Completing tasks					
3.	Conflict resolution					
4.	Collaboration with others					
5.	Organize your time					
6.	Organizing skills					
7.	Putting a positive thing on discussions					
8.	Keeping someone's attention and support					
9.	A review of what was spoken					
10.	Significantly reducing the seriousness of a discussion.					
11.	Increasing the seriousness of a discussion					
12.	Self-disclosure					
13.	Showing your support					
14.	Changing the conversation's focus					
15.	Waiting for answers					

16.	Posing open-ended inquiries					
17.	Clarification					
18.	Providing emotional support and guidance					
19.	Providing details					
20.	Appreciating the sentiments of others					
21.	Dealing with Conversational Silences					
22.	Dealing with apathy and disinterested expressions					
23.	Negative comments and how to respond					
24.	Responding to anxious expressions					
25.	Reacting to compliments					
26.	Managing Anger and Hostility					
27.	Emotion's transmission					
28.	Listening - expressing an interest in others					
29.	Listening, including taking in what others have to say.					

❖ You may average your evaluations to get a total "interpersonal effectiveness" skill grade.

- **Try Not to Listen to Activity**

Encourage the participants to identify a partner with whom they can collaborate. Each individual will take turns talking for two minutes on whatever they want while the other participant clarifies that they are not paying attention. So, let's call them John and Sara, and John speaks for two minutes while Sara shows that she is not listening and cannot say anything. Then they switch places, and it is Sara's time.

When respondents try to talk for two minutes, they usually run out of steam before the end of the time limit. It is tough to keep going when no one pays attention to you. This is a light-hearted beginning to the exercise, so it does not matter if it devolves into the comic mess; the points will still be conveyed.

When both John and Sara have had their time, ask them how it felt not to be listened, and then discuss and write down their instant emotions on the chart paper or board.

The following is a list of the replies they are most likely to give:

- o Frustrated
- o Agitated
- o That I am insignificant
- o It was boring to listen to what I was speaking.
- o I couldn't go on any longer — I'd run out of steam.
- o I felt little and unimportant.

Then inquire about the actions they noticed in the individual who was not paying attention to them.

_____

_____

_____

While this is an overestimate of what it is like to chat to someone who is not paying attention, it can help people who are not attentive or have weak social skills to keep track of their conduct while engaging with others.

Discovering Your Talent

> ✦ I would describe my personality as...

> ✦ Whenever my work or idea gets criticized, I feel like...

> ✦ When I was a child, I loved to...

> ✦ If I am a super wo(man), I will change...

> ✦ I am passionate about...

+ I am very good at...

+ I am very bad at...
+

+ I am struggling with...

+ I maintain my struggling spirits up. Because I am motivated by...

+ If I were the only person on the planet, I would...

+ I feel guilty when I...

+ Through assisting others, I've been able to expand my...

+ Those I've assisted have remarked I'm good at...

+ My difficulties have taught me to...

+ Even though I'm no longer a child, I can't seem to break free from my childhood patterns of...

Examine your responses to the following questions. Concentrate on your responses to identify common ground, then derive your decision from understanding your personality.

- **Sabotage Exercise**

This is another entertaining activity that involves negative interpersonal behaviors to showcase positive interpersonal actions.

This activity should be done in a big group, one that can be divided into at least 2 or 3 groups of 4 to 5 people.

Teach each group to spend about 10 minutes brainstorming, discussing, and listing all possible methods to undermine a collaborative project. Anything they can think of is perfectly acceptable — it just has to be distracting enough to knock a team project off track!

Gather the bigger group and compare replies once each group has a good-sized list of methods to undermine a group project. Put it all on the front of the room's blackboard, whiteboard, or flipping board.

Then, tell the groups to create a 5-to-10-point contract with defined guidelines for effective group work. Members of the group should use the sabotage concepts (that is, things not to do for effective group work) to come up with new ideas (i.e., things to do for effective group work).

Suppose a team listed "do not interact with any of the other team members" as a means to sabotage the group project. In that case, they may come up with "talk with other team members frequently" as a recommendation for effective group work.

This activity will teach participants what makes for a great group experience while simultaneously providing them with the opportunity to have a good group experience.

- **Count the Squares Game (illustrations)**

This game is an interactive and enjoyable method to get people talking and interacting in groups. Allow the group a few minutes to count the number of squares in the image and jot down their answers in the first stage. They should do it without informing anyone else.

Then, have each team member say how many squares they counted. Make a list of them on the whiteboard. Now advise each individual to pick a partner and count the squares once more. They can communicate with each other while considering the number of squares, but not with anybody else. Once they have finished, have each pair disclose their numbers once again.

Attendees will learn the value of excellent group communication, experience working in groups or pairs, and ideally enjoy themselves while doing this exercise.

PUZZLE
How many squares are there?

- **Non-Verbal Introduction Game**

To reap the benefits of engaging each team member, play this game during the first day of group sessions. Assign each group member to a person who will sit beside them. Tell them to identify themselves to one another and include anything unique or fascinating about themselves in their introductions.

Bring the attention back to the bigger group once each pair has been presented and has learned something fascinating about the other. Tell the group that each individual must present their relationship to the rest of the team, but they must do so without using words or props! Each partner must solely use acts to welcome the other.

This game is not only a terrific icebreaker for meeting new people, but it is also a fun method for team members to see the value of oral communication (which you may only realize when you cannot use it!) as well as the significance of nonverbal communication.

The Final Message

This book has a lot of information, and I believe you have found it worthwhile to read. The goal of this book was to give an introduction to Dialectical Behavior Therapy and detail the skills and techniques that may be used to help you or your patients with emotion control concerns. I hope it has accomplished this purpose and that you already know a lot more about Dialectical Behavior Therapy than you knew before!

If you or someone you love is struggling with the pain that comes with a regular lifestyle, this type of therapy has been proven quite effective. It is simpler than ever to try DBT nowadays. DBT can achieve exceptionally beneficial effects in a wide range of people, not only those with mental illnesses. When it comes to mindfulness in DBT, there are a variety of incredible advantages to practicing mindfulness. The justifications for not practicing mindfulness are rapidly disappearing with such promising results.

I have provided you with several exercises and activities for mindfulness, emotional regulation, stress reduction, discovering inner focus, and interpersonal skills worksheets. I hope you will find these strategies and insights as beneficial as I did!

Remember that the techniques taught in DBT are equally useful for those who are not struggling with a mental health problem. Mindfulness, concentrating on the positives, let go of the bad, and embracing the realities of your circumstance are all skills that may assist anybody, not just those who are struggling. This book has given you the tools and information you need to begin with DBT, whether you choose to try it yourself or assist your patients through it.

Have you tried DBT skills to improve your ability to control your emotions? What techniques did you utilize? Would you adopt any of these methods I described here? Please share your comments on Amazon.

Thank you for reading!

Made in the USA
Monee, IL
23 February 2022

91711926R00069